Preparing Future Leaders for Social Justice

Bridging Theory and Practice

This international series reflects the latest cutting-edge theories and practices in school leadership. Uniquely, we include books that bridge the perennial divide between theory and practice. The series motto is framed after Kurt Lewin's famous statement, and we paraphrase that there is no sound theory without practice and no good practice that is not framed on some theory.

Preparing Future Leaders for Social Justice

Bridging Theory and Practice through a Transformative Andragogy

Kathleen M. Brown and Haim Shaked

Series Editor: Jeffrey Glanz

ROWMAN & LITTLEFIELD
Lanham • Boulder • New York • London

Published by Rowman & Littlefield
A wholly owned subsidiary of The Rowman & Littlefield Publishing Group, Inc.
4501 Forbes Boulevard, Suite 200, Lanham, Maryland 20706
www.rowman.com

Unit A, Whitacre Mews, 26–34 Stannary Street, London SE11 4AB

British Library Cataloguing in Publication Information Available

Library of Congress Cataloging-in-Publication Data
Names: Brown, Kathleen M., author.
Title: Preparing future leaders for social justice: bridging theory and practice
    through a transformative andragogy/Kathleen M. Brown and Haim Shaked.
Description: Second Edition. | Lanham, Maryland : Rowman & Littlefield, [2018] |
    Series: Bridging theory and practice | Includes bibliographical references and index.
Identifiers: LCCN 2018022687 (print) | LCCN 2018023564 (ebook) |
    ISBN 9781475845068 (Electronic) | ISBN 9781475845044 (Cloth : alk. paper) |
    ISBN 9781475845051 (Paperback : alk. paper)
Subjects: LCSH: Educational leadership—United States. | School management and
    organization—United States.
Classification: LCC LB2805 (ebook) | LCC LB2805. B824 2018 (print) |
    DDC 371.2—dc23

♾️™ The paper used in this publication meets the minimum requirements of American National Standard for Information Sciences—Permanence of Paper for Printed Library Materials, ANSI/NISO Z39.48–1992.

Printed in the United States of America

Contents

Introduction—Second Edition

In today's Western schools, white, straight, middle-class, and physically able students reach higher achievements and drop out less. They have a greater chance of learning in higher education institutions than their counterparts who do not possess these characteristics (Darling-Hammond, 2010; Sweet, Anisef, Brown, Walters, & Phythian, 2010).

Unfortunately, recent educational policies aimed at narrowing inequality gaps in academic outcomes have hurt the marginalized, particularly the poor and non-white, students more than they did to anyone else (Fabricant & Fine, 2013; Hursh, 2007). These students find themselves in schools stripped of resources, exposed to outdated and inefficient pedagogy, and unjustly held back from progressing, and they are inevitably pushed out of school after having been instructed by teachers who would prefer, if only they could, to work in other schools (Ryan, 2016).

To create a learning climate that provides all students equal opportunity regardless of race, class, gender, physical ability or disability, sexual orientation, and other potentially marginalizing characteristics, we need skilled school leaders. School leadership's effectiveness is crucial to improving student learning, and its greatest impact is felt in schools with the greatest need (Bryk, Sebring, Allensworth, Luppescu, & Easton, 2010; Louis, Leithwood, Wahlstrom, & Anderson, 2010). "Leadership has very significant effects on the quality of school organization and on pupil learning . . . there is not a single documented case of a school successfully turning around its pupil achievement trajectory in the absence of talented leadership" (Leithwood, Harris, & Hopkins, 2008).

The quality of principals' functioning depends to a great extent on the quality of their preparation (Anderson & Reynolds, 2015; Davis & Darling-Hammond, 2012). High-quality preparation experiences could equip preservice principals with strategies that will enable them to transform schools into spaces where all students, without exception, thrive (Lopez, 2010; McKenzie, et al., 2008). However, much of the literature has been critical of how school administrators are prepared (Lynch, 2012; Oplatka & Waite, 2010; Williams, 2015).

Particularly, the existing research dealing with the question of how to prepare social justice school leaders—principals who organize their schools to advance all students' equitable learning—is meager (Guerra, Nelson, Jacobs, & Yamamura, 2013). Hence the importance of this book, which presents an implementable model that addresses the challenges involved in preparing educational leaders for realizing social justice, equality, and excellence in their schools.

The current second edition of this book includes the main parts of its first edition. The original chapters of the book have not been changed. However, in each of the two sections of this book, we have added a chapter covering the latest research, which reviews relevant literature that was published during the years following the publication of the first edition. Given the limited knowledge available regarding the training of educational leaders for social justice, equality, and excellence, this book is of utmost importance, thus deserving of a second edition. It is our hope that it will be used by those who wish to prepare tomorrow's school leaders for their role as promoters of social justice.

REFERENCES

Anderson, E., & Reynolds, A. L. (2015). *A policymaker's guide: Research-based policy for principal preparation program approval and licensure.* Charlottesville, VA: University Council of Educational Administration.

Bryk, A. S., Sebring, P. B., Allensworth, E., Luppescu, S., & Easton, J. Q. (2010). *Organizing schools for improvement: Lessons from Chicago.* Chicago, IL: University of Chicago Press.

Darling-Hammond, L. (2010). *The flat world and education: How America's commitment to equity will determine our future.* New York, NY: Teachers College Press.

Davis, S. H., & Darling-Hammond, L. (2012). Innovative principal preparation programs: What works and how we know. *Planning and Changing, 43*(1–2), 25–45.

Fabricant, M., & Fine, M. (2013). *The changing politics of education: Privatization and the dispossessed lives left behind.* Boulder, CO: Paradigm.

Guerra, P. L., Nelson, S. W., Jacobs, J., & Yamamura, E. (2013). Developing educational leaders for social justice: Programmatic elements that work or need improvement. *Education Research and Perspectives, 40*(1), 124–149.

Hursh, D. (2007). Assessing no child left behind and the rise of neoliberal education policies. *American Educational Research Journal, 44*(3), 493–518.

Leithwood, K., Harris, A., & Hopkins, D. (2008). Seven strong claims about successful school leadership. *School Leadership & Management, 28*(1), 27–42.

Lopez, G. (2010). Mainstreaming diversity? "What'chu talking about, Willis?" *UCEA Review, 51*(3), 6–8.

Louis, K. S., Leithwood, K., Wahlstrom, K. L., & Anderson, L. E. (2010). *Learning from leadership: Investigating the links to improved student learning.* New York, NY: Wallace Foundation.

Lynch, J. M. (2012). Responsibilities of today's principal: Implications for principal preparation programs and principal certification policies. *Rural Special Education Quarterly, 31*(2), 40–47.

McKenzie, K. B., Christman, D. E., Hernandez, F., Fierro, E., Capper, C. A., Dantley, M , González, M. L., et al. (2008). From the field: A proposal for educating leaders for social justice. *Educational Administration Quarterly, 44*(1), 111–138.

Oplatka, I., & Waite, D. (2010). The new principal preparation program model in Israel: Ponderings about practice-oriented principal training. In A. H. Normore (Ed.), *Global perspectives on educational leadership reform: The development and preparation of leaders of learning and learners of leadership—Advances in Educational Administration, Volume 11* (pp. 47–66). Bingley, UK: Emerald Group Publishing.

Ryan, J. (2016). Strategic activism, educational leadership and social justice. *International Journal of Leadership in Education, 19*(1), 87–100.

Sweet, R., Anisef, P., Brown, R., Walters, D., & Phythian, K. (2010). *Post-high school pathways of immigrant youth.* Toronto, Canada: Higher Education Quality Council of Ontario.

Williams, S. M. (2015). The future of principal preparation and principal evaluation: Reflections of the current policy context for school leaders. *Journal of Research on Leadership Education, 10*(3), 222–225.

Introduction—First Edition

While many agree that theory, research, and practice should be intertwined to support the type of schooling (and society) that values rather than marginalizes, few scholars offer groundbreaking, pragmatic approaches to developing truly transformative leaders. From a critical theorist perspective, this book offers a practical, process-oriented model that is responsive to the challenges of preparing educational leaders committed to social justice, equity, and excellence.

Advocates for social justice espouse a theory of social critique, embrace a greater sense of civic duty, and willingly become active agents for meaningful change. The purpose of this book is to inform professors of future leaders of an andragogical strategy aimed at developing such principals and then to encourage those same school leaders to modify the activities described herein for use with their own faculty, staff, and parent groups.

Transformative learning is a process of experiential learning, critical self-reflection, and rationale discourse that can be stimulated by people, events, or changes in context that challenge the learner's basic assumptions of the world. Transformative learning leads to a new way of seeing. "Values are not necessarily changed, but are examined—their source is identified, and they are accepted and justified or revised or possibly rejected" (Cranton, 1992, p. 146).

This in turn leads to some kind of action. By weaving a tripartite theoretical framework together in support of an alternative, transformative andragogy, future leaders can learn "to perceive social, political, and economic contradictions, and to take action against the oppressive elements of reality" (Freire, 1994, p. 17). They can in turn begin to recognize and refine their own agency in teaching and leading others.

Transformative andragogy is the art and science of helping others learn. It is the art and science of helping others to think critically and act responsibly; to examine beliefs; to accept, reject, or modify values; and to engage in activism and advocacy with and for others. As such, the three theoretical perspectives of adult learning theory, transformative learning theory, and critical social theory are interwoven with the three andragogical strategies of critical reflection, rational discourse, and policy praxis to increase adult learners' awareness of self, acknowledgment of others, and action for equity.

In doing so, Giroux (1993) has urged educational leadership faculty to create "a new language capable of asking new questions and generating more critical practices" (p. 37). As such, reflective questions are provided at the end of each chapter to help professors and future principals alike rethink theory and practice; reformulate traditional notions of power, authority, and ethics; and refocus education around concerns of justice, equity, diversity, privilege, student achievement, and social responsibility.

Critical theory is grounded in the day-to-day lives of people, structures, and cultures. It pays attention to the educational ideas, policies, and practices that serve the interests of the dominant class while simultaneously silencing and dehumanizing "others." According to Beyer (2001), "It is precisely in understanding the normative dimensions of education and how they are intertwined with social, structural, and ideological processes and realities that critical theory plays a key role" (p. 154).

A critical stance frames this discussion by outlining clearly the need for professors to retool their teaching and courses to address issues of power and privilege—to weave social justice into the fabric of educational leadership curriculum, pedagogy, programs, and policies. At the same time, it recognizes and advocates for the social change role and responsibility of educational leaders. This book encourages future principals to become more deeply aware of the impact that race, class, gender, sexual orientation, disability, language, immigration, and religion have on schools and students' learning and to commit themselves to challenging systemic inequities and to leading teachers in creating equitable opportunities for all students.

Since contemporary researchers (Argyris, 1990; Banks, 1994; Senge et al., 1994; Wheatley, 1992) have found that effective leaders take responsibility for their learning, share a vision for what can be, assess their own assumptions and beliefs, and understand the structural and organic nature of schools, preparation programs and staff development programs need to carefully craft authentic experiences aimed at developing such skills. Future and current leaders need time to think, reflect, assess, decide, and possibly change. By exposing adult learners to information and ideas that they may resist and by assisting them to stretch beyond their comfort zones, a critique and transformation of hegemonic structures and ideologies can occur.

While the strategies proposed here focus specifically on preservice preparation, their applicability to ongoing professional learning for in-service principals to use with their faculty, staff, and parent groups is an important and necessary complement. The model proposed (see figure A) promotes awareness of self through critical reflection, acknowledgment of others through rational discourse, and action for equity through policy praxis (i.e., reflective practice or a union between thought and action). All three components are necessary in preparing leaders with the knowledge, skill, and desire to examine why and how some school policies and practices "devalue the identities of some students while overvaluing others" (Nieto, 2000, p. 183).

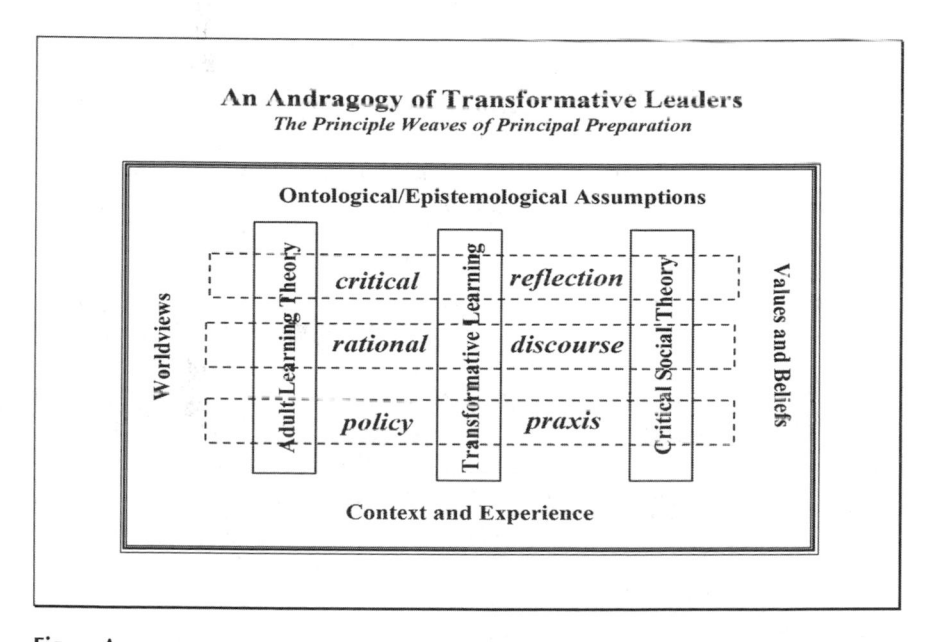

Figure A

This book is divided into two main sections. "Section I: Transformative Ideas and the Contextual Background" contains three chapters that lay the groundwork for preparing leaders for social justice, equity, and excellence. Chapter 1 provides readers with an overview of the role of the principal in actually promoting social justice, equity, and excellence. Although many schools are failing to fulfill their duty, others are meeting the challenge of serving each and every student really well (Oakes et al., 2000; Riester, Pursch, & Skrla, 2002).

The literature on leadership for social justice identifies schools that have demonstrated tremendous success not only with white middle-class and affluent students but also with students from varied racial, socioeconomic, linguistic, and cultural backgrounds (Capper & Young, 2007; Scheurich,

1998). In striving for equity and excellence, virtually all students in these schools are learning at high academic levels. There are "no persistent patterns of differences in academic success or treatment among students grouped by race, ethnicity, culture, neighborhood, income of parents, or home language" (Scheurich & Skrla, 2003, p. 2).

From a critical theorist perspective, chapter 2 then describes a practical, process-oriented model that is responsive to the challenges of preparing such educational leaders committed to social justice, equity, and excellence. This is followed by a mixed-methods research study aimed at documenting theory into practice findings.

Throughout the three chapters in "Section II: Transformative Andragogical Practice and the Centrality of Experience," the three theoretical perspectives of adult learning theory, transformative learning theory, and critical social theory are interwoven with the three andragogical strategies of critical reflection, rational discourse, and policy praxis to increase future and current leaders' awareness, acknowledgment, and action for social justice, equity, and excellence.

Employing a critical, transformative andragogy requires professors and principals to be active facilitators and co-learners who go beyond simply meeting the expressed needs of the learner or the teacher. Through a wide array of roles, methods, and techniques, they need to take on the responsibility for growth by questioning the learner's expectations and beliefs. Transformative learning may occur as a result of a life crisis or may be precipitated by challenging interactions with others, by participation in carefully designed exercises and activities, and by stimulation through reading or other resources.

By being actively engaged in a number of assignments requiring the examination of ontological and epistemological assumptions, values and beliefs, context and experience, and competing worldviews, chapters 4, 5, and 6 demonstrate how adult learners (principals and teachers) can be better equipped to work with and guide others in translating their perspectives, perceptions, and goals into agendas for social change. The exploration of new understandings, the synthesis of new information, and the integration of these insights throughout personal and professional spheres can lead future and current educational leaders and their school faculties to a broader, more inclusive approach in addressing issues of student learning and equity in their schools and districts.

The book concludes with a call for action—a call for social justice, equity, and excellence in U.S. schools, a call for all professors of educational leadership and all school principals to become transformative leaders, a call for all educators to serve as change agents who analyze cultural and political aspects that have permitted long-standing social inequalities to not only proliferate but also become institutional ideological belief systems.

As stated in the introduction to this series, the purpose of this book is "to provide future and current school leaders with the requisite knowledge, skills, and dispositions that promote best practice"—best practice that links educational equity with social equity, best practice that engages the school and community in confronting issues of social justice, best practice that avoids political traps and fights instead for substantive educational improvements for all students so that no child is left behind.

REFERENCES

Argyris, C. (1990). *Overcoming organizational defenses: Facilitating organizational learning.* Englewood Cliffs, NJ: Prentice Hall.

Banks, J. (1994). *Multiethnic education: Theory and practice.* Needham Heights, MA: Allyn & Bacon.

Beyer, L. E. (2001). The value of critical perspectives in teacher education. *Journal of Teacher Education, 52*(2), 151–163.

Capper, C., & Young, M. (2007). *Educational Leaders for Social Justice.* New York, NY: Teachers College Press.

Cranton, P. (1992). *Working with adult learners.* Toronto, Canada: Wall & Emerson.

Freire, P. (1994/1970). *Pedagogy of the oppressed* (Revised edition). New York, NY: Continuum.

Giroux, H. A. (1993). Educational leadership and school administration: Rethinking the meaning of democratic public cultures. In T. A. Mulkeen, N. Cambron-McCabe, & B. J. Anderson (Eds.), *Democratic leadership: The changing context of administrative preparation.* Norwood, NJ: Ablex.

Nieto, S. (2000). Placing equity front and center: Some thoughts on transforming teaching education for a new century. *Journal of Teacher Education, 51*(3), 180–187.

Oakes, J., Quartz, K. H., Ryan, S., & Lipton, M. (2000). Becoming good American schools. *Phi Delta Kappan, 81*(8), 568–576.

Riester, A. F., Pursch, V., & Skrla L. (2002). Principals for social justice: Leaders of school success for children from low-income homes. *Journal of School Leadership, 12*(3), 281–304.

Scheurich, J. J. (1998). Highly successful and loving, public elementary schools populated mainly by low-SES children of color. *Urban Education, 33*, 451–491.

Scheurich, J., & Skrla, L. (2003). *Leadership for equity and excellence: Creating high achievement classrooms, schools, and districts.* Thousand Oaks, CA: Corwin.

Senge, P., Kleiner, A., Roberts, C., Ross, R., & Smith, B. (1994). *The fifth discipline fieldbook: Strategies and tools for building a learning organization.* New York, NY: Doubleday.

Wheatley, M. (1992). *Leadership and the new science.* San Francisco, CA: Berrett-Koehler.

Section I

TRANSFORMATIVE IDEAS AND THE CONTEXTUAL BACKGROUND

Chapter 1

The Principal's Role in Promoting Social Justice, Equity, and Excellence

INTRODUCTION

Despite conflicting views of social justice, of the sources of injustice in schools and society, and of educators' obligations to committed action, the evidence is clear and alarming that various segments of our public school population experience negative and inequitable treatment on a daily basis (Ladson-Billings, 1994; Scheurich & Laible, 1999; Valenzuela, 1999). When compared to their white middle-class counterparts, students of color, students of low socioeconomic status, students who speak languages other than English, and students with disabilities consistently experience significantly lower achievement test scores, teacher expectations, and allocation of resources (Alexander, Entwisle, & Olsen, 2001; Banks, 1997; Delpit, 1995; Jencks & Phillips, 1998; Ortiz, 1997).

Haycock (2001) has maintained that the gaps exist because "we take the students who have less to begin with and then systematically give them less in schools" (p. 8). The differences show up in the curriculum taught, the resources spent, how teachers are assigned, and achievement expected. According to Oakes, Quartz, Ryan, and Lipton (2000), one reason that the "gaps" are so persistent, pervasive, and significantly disparate is that "American schools have been pressured to preserve the status quo" (p. 573).

The historic marginalization of underprivileged students and the perpetuation of the status quo have served to benefit the same students and families for hundreds of years while simultaneously ignoring the needs of low-income, black, brown, native, and Asian students and their families (Apple, 1993; Delpit, 1995; Larson & Ovando, 2001). As a result, these students, without realizing it, fall into a predetermined mold designed for school failure and

3

social inequity. They are "left behind" without hope, without vision, and without equal access to the excellent education that *all* children are entitled.

Freire (1970) proposed that the purpose of our educational system is to make bold possibilities happen for these students. He stated that it is the work, in fact the duty, of public education to end the oppression of these students. Moses (Moses & Cobb, 2002) agreed, suggesting that educators today are actually the frontline civil rights workers in a long-term struggle to increase equity. Although many schools are failing to fulfill this duty, others are meeting the challenge of serving each and every student really well (Oakes et al., 2000; Riester, Pursch, & Skrla, 2002).

The literature on leadership for social justice identifies schools that have demonstrated tremendous success not only with white middle-class and affluent students but also with students from varied racial, socioeconomic, linguistic, and cultural backgrounds (Capper & Young, 2007; Scheurich, 1998). In striving for equity *and* excellence, virtually all students in these schools are learning at high academic levels. There are "no persistent patterns of differences in academic success or treatment among students grouped by race, ethnicity, culture, neighborhood, income of parents, or home language" (Scheurich & Skrla, 2003, p. 2).

This chapter begins by describing the results of several of these studies of "effective, high-performing" schools, pointing to important building-level factors that principals must have in place in order for all children to achieve at high levels. This is followed by a section that highlights the empirical research directly correlating principal leadership to student achievement. The leadership characteristics necessary for truly promoting social justice, equity, and excellence in schools are outlined next. And finally, the factors needed to adequately prepare future leaders for this type of work are discussed.

EFFECTIVE, HIGH-PERFORMING SCHOOLS

The quest for more effective forms of schooling has traditionally been synonymous with the quest for greater educational equity across racial and socioeconomic levels. Beginning with the Coleman Report of the mid-1960s (Coleman et al., 1966), the past 40 years have witnessed a growing number of research studies aimed at reducing the gap in quality between the school experiences of disadvantaged and more affluent youth. These research studies have concluded that the strongest predictors of achievement across all racial groups were social characteristics of the student's home environment (e.g., parents' education, income).

Coleman proposed that children from poor families and homes, lacking the prime conditions or values to support education, could not learn, regardless of what the school did—in essence, absolving schools of the responsibility for student achievement. Through the "effective schools research," Edmunds et al. (see Rosenholtz, 1985) set out to find schools where children from low-income families were highly successful and thereby prove that schools can and do make a difference and that children from poverty backgrounds can learn at high levels.

Many of these process-product studies identified samples of high-performing schools, documenting certain school, classroom, and leadership practices that are critical to enhanced student achievement and school productivity, regardless of family background. These unique characteristics and processes within the purview of schools are correlated with high and equitable levels of student learning.

Summarizing these findings, Odden and Odden (1995) noted that effective teachers maximize instruction time, are well prepared, maintain a smooth and steady instructional pace (especially during the first few weeks of school), focus on academic learning, and emphasize student mastery of material. With regard to organizational characteristics, effective schools evidence strong instructional leadership, usually provided by the principal; a consensus on academically focused school goals; realistic but high expectations for student learning; regularized monitoring of progress toward academic goals; ongoing staff development; and an orderly and secure environment (Odden & Odden, 1995).

Other studies found similar characteristics of a school's climate associated with improved, better student learning. For example, in 1988, Bryk and Driscoll (1988) expanded the notion of school commonality, arguing that "communally organized" schools evidence a consensus over beliefs and values; a "common agenda" of course work, activities, ceremonies, and traditions; and an ethic of caring that pervades the relationships of student and adult school members (also see Noddings, 1992).

On the basis of analyses of a national sample of schools and students, Bryk and Driscoll found that schools with higher levels of commonality (as measured by an array of survey items representing each of the three core components) also evidenced higher attendance rates, better morale (among both students and teachers), and higher levels of student achievement. Shouse's 1996 follow-up study separately examined the achievement effects of commonality (measured along lines similar to those of Bryk and Driscoll's study) and "academic press" (measured in terms of an assortment of survey items reflecting school academic climate, disciplinary climate, and teachers' instructional behavior and emphasis).

The findings revealed that academic effectiveness among low-socioeconomic status (low-SES) schools was significantly tied to academic press and to an integrated culture of academic press and commonality. Average achievement in low-SES schools having high levels of both academic press and commonality rivaled that of schools serving more affluent students. Conversely, the least academically effective low-SES schools were those that combined strong commonality and weak academic press. Although these findings reveal the tensions between meeting students' social and academic needs, they also reveal the tremendous potential of school social networks that are supportive, cohesive, and academically oriented to greatly enhance the quality of urban students' educational experiences (Shouse, 1996).

Similar to the effective schools movement, the school restructuring movement also denotes a fairly specific array of prescriptions for improving organizational effectiveness and student achievement. The tenets offered by this movement center around three basic areas: (1) shifting the thrust of school governance to a more "bottom-up" direction through decentralization, site-based management, staff professional development, teacher empowerment, and greater parent involvement; (2) refocusing curriculum and instruction toward cooperatively organized, mixed-ability classrooms, greater emphasis on higher-order learning, and the use of performance-based student assessment; and (3) reducing school size, typically through the creation of "schools within schools."

Research evidence links the collective adoption of these areas with significant gains in high school achievement. A study by Lee and Smith (1994), for example, contrasted achievement gains in three types of school: (1) those with no reform or restructuring; (2) those that had sought to improve on their traditional, more bureaucratic practices; and (3) those that had engaged in some level of organizational restructuring.

Although students in traditionally oriented schools that were seeking improvement outgained those in nonreform schools, students in restructured schools (those having adopted at least three out of twelve restructuring practices) significantly outgained those in both other types of schools (Lee & Smith, 1994). More important, the achievement gap between more and less economically advantaged students was narrowest within restructured schools.

Significant, collective involvement of teachers also appears to be a key to effective school restructuring. Researchers found that school effectiveness and student learning were enhanced when schools took on the qualities of "professional communities" (Louis & Kruse, 1995; Newmann & Wehlage, 1995). Such communities had the following three basic features: "Teachers pursue a clear shared purpose for all students' learning. Teachers engage in collaborative activity to achieve the purpose. Teachers take collective responsibility for student learning" (Newmann & Wehlage, 1995, p. 30).

In effective schools, which typically operate as strong professional learning communities, Fullan (2000) found that teachers systematically study student assessment data, relate the data to their instruction, and work with others to refine their teaching practices. Louis and Kruse (1995) concur, claiming that reflective dialogue, deprivatization of practice, and collaborative efforts all enhance shared understandings and strengthen relationships within a school.

Barth (1990) added that a "good school . . . is a place where everyone is teaching and everyone is learning—simultaneously, under the same roof" (p. 163). He writes that the adults enter into a collaborative relationship and create an "ecology of reflection, growth, and refinement of practice" (p. 162). Such communities promote purposeful and collaborative classrooms among teachers, administrators, and parents to improve instruction; create with others climate of care; and use accountability to continuously scan for inequities across multiple domains of student learning and activities.

In recent years, a revival of effective schools research has surfaced, most likely due to widespread national concerns about student achievement. Such research has shifted in emphasis over the years, from economic to structural and on to social models of urban school effectiveness, from highlighting school funding and physical resources to teachers' instructional behaviors and on to a school's sense of community and academic culture. For example, a recent study of highly effective schools in New York City (Teske & Schneider, 1999) suggests that within these schools, there is a culture defined and sustained by a combination of strong, consistent leadership and strong community support.

Another study by Taylor, Pressley, and Pearson (2002) summarized findings from five large-scale research studies on effective, high-poverty elementary schools (Charles A. Dana Center, 1999; Designs for Change, 1998; Lein, Johnson, & Ragland, 1997; Puma et al., 1997; Taylor, Pearson, Clark, & Walpole, 2000). The six recurring themes that emerged from these five studies support and extend the earlier research on effective schools: (1) putting the students first to improve students' learning, (2) strong building-level leadership, (3) strong teacher collaboration, (4) focus on professional development and innovation, (5) consistent use of student performance data to improve learning, and (6) strong links to parents. Such research stresses the importance of educators (teachers and principals) learning and changing together over an extended period of time, as they reflect on their practice and implement new teaching strategies (Fullan & Hargreaves, 1996).

While the effective schools movement has been influential among researchers, educators, and policymakers, questions persist regarding its various recommendations, particularly the direction of causal effect. In other words, although certain characteristics might produce higher-achieving students, the reverse might also be the case; that is, schools may maintain these characteristics because they are fortunate enough to have greater numbers of high-achieving students. That some schools identified as effective at one point in time were found not to be so a few years later might, for example, suggest the latter possibility. Thus, although "effective schools" clearly share important practices, it has never been consistently established that ineffective schools could become more effective by adopting these features.

Still unattained and perplexing is the crucial research goal of establishing a reliable set of techniques for transforming ineffective schools into effective ones. In that challenge, effective leadership becomes paramount to schools as they answer the call for accountability and continuously improve the quality of students' educational experiences. As such, the next section emphasizes the critical role of principal leadership as related to students' academic success.

PRINCIPAL LEADERSHIP AND STUDENT ACHIEVEMENT

Although current school reform efforts use different approaches to improve teaching and learning, all depend on the motivation and capacities of local leadership for their success. According to Fullan (2005), "Leadership is to the current decade what standards were to the 1990s for those interested in large scale reform. Standards, even when well implemented, can take us only part way to successful large-scale reform. It is only leadership that can take us all the way" (p. 32). A review of the literature on school reform and restructuring confirms the notion that the school principal is indeed the key player in all successful school reform efforts and that good teaching is not the only predictor of student success—leadership becomes an important lever for improving student achievement.

The belief in the principal's influence on student achievement goes back to the research of the 1970s and early 1980s. Two decades ago, the education report "A Nation at Risk" (National Commission on Excellence in Education, 1983) specifically recommended strong leadership as a means for school improvement. Effective schools research also recognized the importance of quality leadership by consistently identifying strong instructional leadership as instrumental in creating a positive school climate and as a correlate of high-achieving schools (Edmonds, 1979). In schools where students performed better than expected in spite of poverty and other demographic characteristics, a "dynamic" principal was at the helm.

These studies suggested that specific actions by principals could directly influence student achievement. Even though this is an assumption, there is little evidence to support the idea that student achievement has increased as the result of principals' direct actions in instructional supervision. Current theory and research evidence point toward principals affecting student achievement indirectly, through teachers and staff members. As with any manager or leader, principals influence performance through others, and the influence includes a broad spectrum of behaviors.

Although it is difficult to demonstrate a direct link between school leadership and student achievement (the most tangible and publicly accepted measure of school success), a model of what makes a good leader is emerging. A recent forum of the National Institute on Educational Governance, Finance, Policymaking, and Management (1999) developed a comprehensive description of an effective school leader. Consistent with the observation that the job of a school leader is multidimensional, the forum identified areas in which school leaders must have skills: instructional leadership; management; communication, collaboration, and community building; and vision development, risk-taking, and change management.

In other studies that document the importance of strong building leadership (Designs for Change, 1998; Lein et al., 1997; Puma et al., 1997), principals worked to redirect people's time and energy, to develop a collective sense of responsibility for school improvement, to secure resources and training, to provide opportunities for collaboration, to create additional time for instruction, and to help the school staff persist in spite of difficulties. While their style and roles may be different, effective leaders create a culture for school improvement. They understand that "although leadership can be a powerful force toward school reform, the notion that an individual can effect change by sheer will and personality is simply not supported by research" (Marzano, 2003, p. 174). As a result, they promote the involvement of teachers and parents in the decision-making process and are not threatened by, but rather welcome, this empowerment.

Research conducted by Andrews and Soder (1987), Bender Sebring and Bryk (2000), and Hallinger, Bickman, and Davis (1996) found that high-performing schools that demonstrate better student achievement possess a climate that focuses on student learning. Principals in these schools provide clarity to the school's mission, which influences everyone's expectations; have a vision that they allow staff and parents to shape; hold teachers and themselves to high standards; recognize student achievement; communicate academic achievements to the community; and encourage teachers to take risks in trying new methods and programs.

These research studies also found that schools with effective principals exhibit a sense of teamwork and inclusiveness in planning, enabling, and assessing instruction. Principals in these schools involve teachers in instructional decisions, provide opportunities for staff members and parents to assume leadership roles in charting instructional improvement, protect staff members from the community and central office, act as facilitators for the instruction staff, help staff members succeed, serve as an instructional resource for staff members, and create a feeling of trust through cooperative working relationships among the staff in the school. And, according to these research studies, staff members must receive the necessary materials, equipment, and opportunities to learn in order to be successful.

Principals in these schools get things done; assume the role of providing the resources that teachers need; provide staff development to support the staff's efforts to improve; are visible in classrooms, in departmental or grade-level meetings, and in the building; and provide the social support needed by students so that class time is devoted to learning (Andrews & Soder, 1987; Bender Sebring & Bryk, 2000; Hallinger, Bickman, & Davis, 1996).

Since 1998, Mid-continent Research for Education and Learning researchers have been engaged in what they refer to as "third-generation" effective schools research, distinguishing it from the efforts in the 1980s to implement the research findings of the 1970s (see Waters & Grubb, 2004). Recently, they reviewed over 5,000 studies through a series of meta-analyses of research on the student characteristics, school practices, and teacher practices associated with student achievement.

The third meta-analysis focused on the effects of principal leadership on student achievement and involved 70 empirically sound research studies, 2,894 schools, over one million students, and 14,000 teachers, representing the largest sample of principals, teachers, and student achievement scores ever used to analyze the effects of educational leadership. The results show a significant, positive impact of instructional leadership on student achievement (i.e., the study found that the average effect size, expressed as a correlation between leadership and student achievement, is 0.25). The analysis also identified 66 leadership practices embedded in 21 leadership responsibilities, each with statistically significant relationship to student achievement (see table 1.1 for the top 10 principal leadership responsibilities).

Therefore, leadership not only matters, but also according to the Wallace Foundation's "Learning from Leadership Project" (Leithwood, Seashore Louis, Anderson, & Wahlstrom, 2005), school leadership is second only to teacher quality among school-related factors that affect student learning. In a five-year study involving 180 schools, in 45 districts and 9 states, this study attempts to clearly understand the links between student outcomes and the work of principals and other educational leaders.

As a precursor to the project, a publication entitled "How Leadership Influences Student Learning" (Leithwood, Seashore-Louis, Anderson, & Wahlstrom, 2004), has been produced. The authors provide an overview of existing research and present the basics of successful leadership. They suggest that across many different settings, three sets of practices make up the basic core of successful leadership: (1) setting direction, (2) developing people, and (3) redesigning the organization. These authors conclude that "the total (direct and indirect) effects of leadership on student learning account for about a quarter of the total school effects" (Leithwood et al., 2005, p. 3). They also found that

Table 1.1   Top 10 Principal Leadership Responsibilities: Average r and Associated Practices

Responsibility	Definition: The extent to which the principal	Avg r 20	Associated practices	No. of schools	No. of studies
Situational awareness	is aware of the details and undercurrents in the running of the school and uses this information to address current and potential problems.	0.33	• Is aware of informal groups and relationships among teachers and staff • Is aware of issues in the school that have not surfaced but could create discord • Can predict what could go wrong from day to day	91	5
Intellectual stimulation	ensures that faculty and staff are aware of the most current theories and practices and makes the discussion of these a regular aspect of the school's culture.	0.32	• Stays informed about current research and theory regarding effective schooling • Continually exposes teachers and staff to cutting-edge ideas about how to be effective • Systematically engages teachers and staff in discussions about current research and theory • Continually involves teachers and staff in reading articles and books about effective practices	321	5
Change agent	is willing to and actively challenges the status quo.	0.30	• Consciously challenges the status quo • Is comfortable leading change initiatives with uncertain outcomes • Systematically considers new and better ways of doing things	479	7

(Continued)

Table 1.1. (Continued)

Responsibility	Definition: The extent to which the principal	Avg r 20	Associated practices	No. of schools	No. of studies
Input	involves teachers in the design and implementation of important decisions and policies.	0.30	• Provides opportunities for input from teachers and staff on all important decisions • Provides opportunities for teachers and staff to be involved in policy development • Involves the school leadership team in decision-making	504	13
Culture	fosters shared beliefs and a sense of community and cooperation.	0.29	• Promotes cooperation among teachers and staff • Promotes a sense of well-being • Promotes cohesion among teachers and staff • Develops an understanding of purpose • Develops a shared vision of what the school could be like	709	13
Monitors/Evaluates	monitors the effectiveness of school practices and their impact on student learning.	0.28	• Monitors and evaluates the effectiveness of the curriculum • Monitors and evaluates the effectiveness of instruction • Monitors and evaluates the effectiveness of assessment	1071	30
Outreach	is an advocate or spokesperson for the school to all stakeholders.	0.28	• Advocates on behalf of the school in the community • Interacts with parents in ways that enhance their support for the school • Ensures that the central office is aware of the school's accomplishments	478	14

Responsibility	Definition: The extent to which the principal	Avg r 20	Associated practices	No. of schools	No. of studies
Order	establishes a set of standard operating principles and procedures.	0.26	• Provides and enforces clear structures, rules, and procedures for teachers, staff, and students • Establishes routines regarding the running of the school that teachers and staff understand and follow • Ensures that the school is in compliance with district and state mandates	456	17
Resources	provides teachers with the material and professional development necessary for the successful execution of their jobs.	0.26	• Ensures that teachers and staff have necessary materials and equipment • Ensures that teachers have necessary professional development opportunities that directly enhance their teaching	570	17
Ideals/beliefs	communicates and operates from strong ideals and beliefs about schooling	0.25	• Holds strong professional ideals and beliefs about schooling, teaching, and learning • Shares ideals and beliefs about schooling, teaching, and learning with teachers, staff, and parents • Demonstrates behaviors that are consistent with ideals and beliefs	526	8

Note: N is population size and r is correlation coefficient

leadership's demonstrated impact tends to be considerably greater in schools where the learning needs are most acute. In essence, the greater the challenge, the greater the impact of leaders' actions on learning.

Reminded by Crawford (1998) that "almost all educational reform efforts have come to the conclusion that the nation cannot attain excellence in education without effective school leadership" (p. 8), principals automatically become essential figures in terms of schoolwide change, priorities, and vision (Blackmore, 2002; Fullan, 1993; Riester, Pursch, & Skrla, 2002; Shields, Larocque, & Oberg, 2002). Strong, outstanding leadership is necessary to any significant transformation of any organization, schools included (Glickman, 2002). As such, exemplary leadership helps point to the necessity for change and helps make the realities of change happen (Bell, Jones, & Johnson 2002; Bogotch, 2002; Grogan, 2002; Rapp, 2002; Solomon, 2002). Leaders for excellence and equity leverage changes in daily practice, making small changes in the structure that begin to transform the system.

LEADERSHIP FOR SOCIAL JUSTICE, EQUITY, AND EXCELLENCE

According to Educational Research Service (1998), the United States is experiencing a dearth of interested, willing, and qualified school leader candidates because the principal today is confronted with a job filled with conflict, ambiguity, and work overload. Given this, it's understandable that fewer and fewer qualified people aspire to the principalship, that good people are becoming increasingly harder to find, and that "bright, young administrators aren't appearing on the horizon" (McCormick, 1987, p. 4). What are the realities of the job? Charged with the mission of improving education for all children (i.e., universal proficiency embodied most recently by the No Child Left Behind Act), the principalship has become progressively more and more demanding and fraught with fragmentation, variety, and brevity (Petersen, 1982).

The role of school leadership has broadened from performing customary administrative and managerial duties—such as budget oversight, operations, and discipline—to include emphasis on other responsibilities such as curriculum development, data analysis, and instructional leadership. According to Murphy and Beck (1994), principals fill a role replete with contradictory demands. They are expected to "work actively to transform, restructure and redefine schools while they hold organizational positions historically and traditionally committed to resisting change and maintaining stability" (p. 3).

There are principals who are facing these challenges every day, and despite countervailing pressures, they resist, survive, and transform schools (Riester, Pursch, & Skrla, 2002; Scheurich, 1998). They enact resistance against the historic marginalization of particular students and resist the pressures pushing schools toward a deceptive caring versus academic culture, or possibly a defeatist apathetic culture.

These leaders, according to Rapp (2002), are willing and able to "leave the comforts and confines of professional codes and state mandates for the riskier waters of higher moral callings" (p. 233). They understand that leadership depends upon relationships and shared values between leaders and followers (Burns, 1978). They also understand that not reflecting on, discussing, and/ or addressing issues of race, poverty, and disability only further perpetuates the safeguarding of power and the status quo (Larson & Murtadha, 2002; Larson & Ovando, 2001). In response, researchers such as Purpel (1989), Shapiro and Stefkovich (2001), Starratt (2003), and others are strongly advocating for ethical leadership.

For example, Andrews and Grogan (2001) specifically call for aspiring principals to "understand their ethical and moral obligations to create schools that promote and deliver social justice" (p. 24). Foster (2004) also calls leaders to serve as change agents who analyze the cultural aspects that have permitted long-standing social inequalities not only to proliferate but also to become institutional ideological belief systems. The question of how to accomplish this remains unanswered.

Given the strong connection between quality principals and high-performing schools, Scheurich and Skrla (2003) claim that "good leadership, the bodies and spirits of our leadership, is crucial to the justice of our cause for equity and excellence in schooling" (p. 99). Effective instructional and administrative leadership helps point to the necessity for change and is required to implement the change processes (Blackmore, 2002; Bogotch, 2002; Fullan, 1993; Rapp, 2002).

Effective leaders are reflective, are proactive, and seek the help that is needed. They nurture an instructional program and school culture conducive to learning and professional growth. They model the values and beliefs important to the institution, hire compatible staff, and face conflict rather than avoid it. They make the shift from personal awareness to social action (Freire, 1973), realizing that respect for diversity entails advocacy, solidarity, an awareness of societal structures of oppression, and critical social consciousness.

Leaders committed to this agenda decide they can create both equitable and excellent schools and then use their time and energy to figure out how to do so. They find a way "for all students to achieve high levels of academic success, regardless of any student's race, ethnicity, culture, neighborhood, income of parents, or home language" (Scheurich & Skrla, 2003, p. 3). In their schools, there is no discernable difference in academic success and treatment among different groups of students. They believe that equity and excellence are the same.

Although studies have examined schools that make a difference in the lives of marginalized children (Oakes, Quartz, Ryan, & Lipton, 2000; Riester, Pursch, & Skrla, 2002), there is an absence of literature regarding principals as the unit of analysis and the process of actually leading for social justice. Related to this is an absence of documented strategies that principals who are leading for equity and excellence use to advance their work in the face of countervailing pressures of public schools.

How do future leaders, who are dedicated to and passionate about social justice and equity, actually carry out their work in the face of resistance? How do future leaders lead schools that are both equitable and excellent? How do they lead schools in which the dream of equity comes alive on an everyday basis through the work of ordinary, everyday people, principals who have narrowed and will eventually eliminate the achievement gaps? How do principals, who study and challenge the very beliefs, attitudes, and practices that keep all children from learning and who no longer tolerate inequities of achievement in their schools, create schools, educational methods, programs, and expectations that have significantly advanced the educational achievements of all students? Such leaders take a stance; they believe that all children can learn to achieve high, predetermined standards, and they make that belief the practice of their work.

PREPARING FUTURE LEADERS FOR SOCIAL JUSTICE, EQUITY, AND EXCELLENCE

If current and future educational leaders are to foster successful, equitable, and socially responsible learning and accountability practices for *all* students, then substantive changes in educational leadership preparation and professional development programs are required. New understandings of leadership and redesigns of such programs have sparked much-needed debate regarding the knowledge base, course offerings, and foundational purpose of educational administration (see Donmoyer, 1999; English, 2000; Murphy, 1999). In fact, recent conversations and presentations at the annual conferences of the American Educational Research Association and the University Council of Educational Administration have identified social justice as a new anchor for the entire profession, servant leadership as a new metaphor, and equity for *all* as a new mantra.

In a paper for the National Commission for the Advancement of Educational Leadership Preparation, Jackson (2001) reviewed innovative and exceptional programs and mentioned the use of cohorts and problem-based learning (see Bridges & Hallinger, 1995) as two instructional strategies worth merit. She also reported, "Issues that did not appear as dominant in these programs as one would expect are those of social justice, equity, excellence, and equality. These are areas that warrant our serious attention especially in light of the changing demographics of our schools" (Jackson, 2001, p. 18).

Research and shifts in the profession agree. One might think that issues of such great concern would be highly visible in the preparation of school leaders, but Henze Katz, Norte, Sather and Walker (2002) learned that "while diversity is given a certain degree of lip service in administrative credentialing programs, these leaders had not been prepared with tools to analyze racial or ethnic conflict, or with specific strategies for building positive interethnic communities" (p. 4). Results from Lyman and Villani's (2002) national survey indicate a similar void—only 14.3 percent of the respondents perceive social justice to be receiving the "most emphasis" in their preparation programs.

The movement from a "community of sameness" to a "community of difference" (see Furman, 1998; Murtadha-Watts, 1999; Shields & Seltzer, 1997) underscores the urgent need to confront socially difficult topics with respect; dialogue; and a continuous expansion of awareness, acknowledgment, and action. Developing the vocabulary, skills, and knowledge necessary to engage in substantive discussions regarding the dynamics of difference is a critical component to the preparation of leaders for social justice, equity, and excellence.

> Wise educational leaders will learn to create psychological spaces for genuine exploration of difference; they will initiate conversations where problems and challenges may be identified and discussed; and they will create a climate in which staff and students feel safe in clarifying their assumptions to deal with cultural dissonance. (Shields, Larocque, & Oberg, 2002, p. 130)

While Andrews and Grogan (2001) call for aspiring principals to "understand their ethical and moral obligations to create schools that promote and deliver social justice" (p. 24), the question of how to accomplish this remains unanswered. If "leadership is the enactment of values" (Miron, 1996), then it makes sense for preparation programs to include approaches that enable participants to challenge their own assumptions; clarify and strengthen their own values; and work on aligning their own behaviors and practice with these beliefs, attitudes, and philosophies.

One problem is that most college faculty who are attempting to teach for and about social justice, however, have not had professional development that specifically prepares them to do so (Bell, Washington, Weinstein, & Love, 1997). For example, when describing their experiences with teaching courses in diversity, four professors at the University of Dayton reported being both stunned and reassured by their students and themselves. "We're convinced that these issues need center stage in our program . . . we wonder whether we as a faculty have committed ourselves to looking at our own attitudes and our own racism and sexism" (Ridenour, First, Lydon, & Partlow, 2001, p. 162).

If the field of educational administration is really serious about preparing leaders conscious of and committed to diminishing the inequities of American life, then the current models of preparation are not up to the task. While the related literature supports the more recent and not-so-traditional delivery methods of clinical experiences, internships, cohort groups, case studies, and problem-based learning, the instructional approach presented here moves far beyond knowledge acquisition at the formal cognitive level.

More alternative approaches focused on skill and attitude development, such as cultural autobiographies, oral life histories, prejudice reduction workshops, cross-cultural interviews, educational plunges, diversity panels, reflective analysis journals, and activist assignments at the micro, meso, and macro levels (see chapters 4, 5, and 6), can help future leaders and professors develop their capacity to reflect and act more effectively.

Several years ago, Scheurich and Laible (1999) asked the important social justice questions facing educational administration professors: "Are we willing to (a) recognize the enormously destructive effects of race, gender, and class biases on our children; (b) commit to decreasing and eventually eradicating these effects; (c) radically change our preparation programs to accomplish this purpose; and (d) follow through long enough to see real changes in our schools?" (p. 319). Unfortunately, research suggests that leadership preparation programs are not heeding this call to action, nor are they adequately meeting the needs of the twenty-first century leader (Hale & Moorman, 2003). Instead, preparation programs are reluctant to engage in substantial programmatic modifications in terms of curriculum or pedagogy.

For example, McCarthy (1999) claims that despite the continuous evolution and the tremendous demands on the role of the school leader, patterns in the training of educational leaders have remained essentially unchanged for decades. Likewise, Hess and Kelly (as cited in Cambron-McCabe & McCarthy, 2005) point out that although leadership expectations for conditions relative to social justice and equity have increased significantly in recent years, leadership preparation programs persist in training for traditional educational environments. As a result, most educational administration training is not focused on understanding the inequities of our society, nor is it focused on preparing principals to engage in social justice or equity work (Bell, Jones, & Johnson, 2002; Brown, 2004; Lyman & Villani, 2002; Marshall, 2004; Rapp, 2002; Rusch, 2004).

Employing a critical, transformative andragogy requires professors to be active facilitators and co-learners who go beyond simply meeting the expressed needs of the learner. Through a wide array of roles, methods, and techniques, they need to take on the responsibility for growth by questioning the learner's expectations and beliefs. Transformative learning is a process of critical self-reflection that can be stimulated by people, events, or changes in context, which challenge the learner's basic assumptions of the world. Cranton (1992) reported that through transformative learning "values are not necessarily changed, but are examined—their source is identified, and they are accepted and justified or revised or possibly rejected" (p. 146).

Transformative learning may occur as a result of a life crisis or may be precipitated by challenging interactions with others, by participation in carefully designed exercises and activities, and by stimulation through reading or other resources. By being actively engaged in a number of assignments requiring the examination of ontological and epistemological assumptions, values and beliefs, context and experience, and competing worldviews, adult learners are better equipped to work with and guide others in translating their perspectives, perceptions, and goals into agendas for social change. The exploration of new understandings, the synthesis of new information, and the integration of these insights throughout personal and professional spheres can lead future educational leaders to a broader, more inclusive approach in addressing issues of student learning and equity.

As moral stewards, school leaders are much more heavily invested in "purpose-defining" activities (Harlow, 1962, p. 61) and in "reflective analysis and . . . active intervention" (Bates, 1984, p. 268) than simply managing existing arrangements (i.e., maintaining the status quo). In fact, Murphy (2001) has recently criticized traditional approaches as "bankrupt" and has recommended recasting preparation around the purposes of leadership. For this to happen, future leaders need to open their minds (see Rokeach, 1960) and explore their self-understandings that are systematically embedded in mind-sets, worldviews, values, and experiences.

According to Senge (1990), these can be seen as mental models and are "deeply ingrained assumptions, generalizations, or even pictures and images that influence how we understand the world and how we take action" (p. 8). As such they resemble what Schon (1987) talked about as a professional's "repertoire." Reminded by Delpit (1995) that we do not really see through our eyes or hear through our ears, but through our beliefs, the internal courage to look within and honestly confront one's biases and shortcomings is necessary in order for the external work in the school community to be authentic and effective. Preparation programs can foster such critical "capacity building" (see Fullan, 1993) through critical reflection, rational discourse, and policy praxis.

Developing leaders for social justice, equity, and excellence requires a deep-seated commitment on the part of preparation programs. It also requires a fundamental rethinking of content, delivery, and assessment. Courses fashioned and infused with critically reflective curricula and methodologies, which stimulate students to think beyond current behavioral and conceptual boundaries in order to study, research, and implement leadership practices fundamentally and holistically, change schools in ways and in manners that are consistent with an equitable, inclusive vision.

The implementation of such strategies is not relevant in all adult education settings, nor is it threat-free. Transformative learning actually poses threats to psychological security as it challenges comfortably established beliefs and values, including those that may be central to self-concept. Transformative learning can also precipitate changes in long-established and cherished relationships (Mezirow, 1990). Because such issues are volatile and frightening, professional development needs to be carefully planned over a series of sessions, with adequate opportunities for debriefing, in a structured setting where people adhere to agreed-on guidelines for safety and confidentiality.

Aware of the potential for surfacing conflict, professors are wise to remember, "Conflict, if respected, is positively associated with creative breakthroughs under complex, turbulent conditions" (Fullan, 1999, p. 22). Although many of us do not feel comfortable and/or capable of dealing with emotionally laden issues that may arise during these experiences, Harrison and Hopkins (1967) noted that "by sidestepping direct, feeling-level involvement with issues and persons, one fails to develop the 'emotional muscle' needed to handle effectively a high degree of emotional impact and stress" (p. 440). Given new roles, changing school demographics, and heightened expectations, principals need "emotional muscle" for interpersonal dynamics, and preparation programs need to foster it!

For this type of work, an integration of social justice and equity issues throughout a range of courses is recommended. The trends in educational studies, as well as the social and academic goals of education, are investigated and viewed from a variety of angles in several different courses so that a deeper understanding may be achieved. Future leaders are encouraged to ponder big-picture, philosophical, legal, and ethical questions. What is the purpose of basic, K–12 schooling? Who is to be served by the educational system? How are the themes of "control" and "cultural domination" played out throughout the history of education in the United States? Are the themes of institutional, cultural, and personal oppression still relevant today? What are the roles and issues facing educational leaders in our schools and in our society?

Courses designed for individuals preparing for careers as transformative educational administrators require critical thought and systematic reflection regarding ideas, values, and beliefs surrounding social life, cultural identity, educational reform, and historical practices. Adult learners are challenged to explore these constructs from numerous, diverse, changing perspectives. Personal biases and preconceived notions they hold about people who are different from themselves by race, ethnicity, culture, gender, socioeconomic class, sexual orientation, and physical and mental abilities are identified and discussed.

It is important to bridge theory and practice, to make connections between course material and the broader social context, to explain to future administrators how they might take an active part in bringing about social change, and to validate and incorporate with course content adult learners' personal knowledge and experience. According to Daresh (2002), a leader's "personal formation," that is, his or her integration of personal and professional knowledge, can provide a moral compass for navigating the complex landscape of practice. As such, these courses require an active, sustained engagement in the subject matter and an openness of mind and heart.

CONCLUSION

Because the "gaps" are persistent, pervasive, and significantly disparate, many scholars (see Cochran-Smith et al., 1999; Grogan, 2002; Kincheloe & Steinberg, 1995; Shields & Oberg, 2000) advocate a critique of educational systems in terms of access, power, and privilege based on race, culture, gender, sexual orientation, language, background, ability, and/or socioeconomic position. In fact, according to Skrla, Scheurich, Johnson, and Koschoreck (2001), "What is critically needed is real-life, context-specific, tactical, antiracist work in our schools" (p. 239). Given this goal, the questions remain— Who? When? Where? How?

According to Leithwood et al. (2005), "We need to be developing leaders with large repertoires of practices and the capacity to choose from that repertoire as needed, not leaders trained in the delivery of one 'ideal' set of practices" (p. 8). Larson and Murtadha (2002) agree, stating that leaders today need to create and maintain alternative, unconventional, and caring constructions of leadership. Hopefully this book will help future and current leaders develop the skills needed to really lead for social justice, equity, and excellence.

CRITICAL QUESTIONS

1. Have American schools been pressured to preserve the status quo? Why/ why not? How? Interrogate how such intersecting forces as capitalism, colonization, and imperialism work to maintain the status quo by silencing, closeting, and effacing differences in terms of race, class, gender, sexuality, ability, language, and religion. What is the meaning of hegemony?

2. *Do standards and high-stakes testing promote or inhibit equity in schools? Why/why not? How? Provide one concrete example demonstrating how standards and/or testing actually helped to increase equity within a school and one concrete example demonstrating how standards and/or testing actually hindered equity within a school. Compare, contrast, deconstruct, and debate the two examples.*
3. *Is it really possible to serve each and every student really well? Why/why not? Is it desirable? Why/why not? Should educators assume the role of civil rights workers? Why/why not?*

REFERENCES

Alexander, K. L., Entwisle, D. R., & Olsen, L.S. (2001). Schools, achievement and inequality: A seasonal perspective. *Education Evaluation and Policy Analysis*, *23*(2), 171–191.

Andrews, R., & Grogan, M. (2001, August). *Defining preparation and professional development for the future*. A paper commissioned for the First Meeting of the National Commission for the Advancement of Educational Leadership Preparation. Racine, WI.

Andrews, R., & Soder, R. (1987). Principal leadership and student achievement. *Educational Leadership*, *44*, 9–11.

Apple, M. W. (1993). *Official knowledge: Democratic education in a conservative age*. New York, NY: Routledge.

Banks, J. (1997). *Educating citizens in a multicultural society*. New York, NY: Teachers College.

Barth, R. (1990). *Improving schools from within: Teachers, parents, and principals can make a difference*. San Francisco, CA: Jossey-Bass.

Bates, R. J. (1984). Toward a critical practice of educational administration. In T. J. Sergiovanni & J. E. Corbally (Eds.), *Leadership and organizational culture: New perspectives on administrative theory and practice* (pp. 260–274). Urbana, IL: University of Illinois.

Bell, G. C., Jones, E. B., & Johnson, J. F. (2002). School reform: Equal expectations on an uneven playing field. *Journal of School Leadership*, *12*(3), 317–336.

Bell, L. A., Washington, S., Weinstein, G., & Love, B. (1997). Knowing ourselves as instructors. In M. Adams, L. A. Bell, and P. Griffin (Eds.), *Teaching for diversity and social justice*. (pp. 299–310). New York, NY: Routledge.

Bender Sebring, P., & Bryk, A. (2000). School leadership and the bottom line in Chicago. *Phi Delta Kappan*, *81*, 440–449.

Blackmore, J. (2002). Leadership for socially just schooling: More substance and less style in high risk, low trust times? *Journal of School Leadership*, *12*(2), 198–222.

Bogotch, I. (2002). Educational leadership and social justice: Practice into theory. *Journal of School Leadership*, *12*(2), 138–156.

Bridges, E. M., & Hallinger, P. (1995). *Problem-based learning in leadership development*. Eugene, OR: ERIC Clearinghouse on Educational Management.

Brown, K. (2004). Leadership for social justice and equity: Weaving a transformative framework and pedagogy. *Educational Administration Quarterly, 40*(1), 79–110.

Bryk, A. S., & Driscoll, M. E. (1988). *The school as community: Theoretical foundations, contextual influences, and consequences for students and teachers.* Chicago, IL: University of Chicago, Benton Center for Curriculum and Instruction.

Burns, J. M. (1978). *Leadership.* New York, NY: Harper Row.

Cambron-McCabe, N., & McCarthy, M. (2005, January). Educating school leaders for social justice. *Educational Policy, 19*(1), 201–222.

Capper, C. A. & Young, M. (2007). *Educational leaders for social justice.* New York, NY: Teacher College.

Charles A. Dana Center, University of Texas at Austin (1999) *Hope for urban education: A study of nine high-performing, high-poverty urban elementary schools.* Washington, DC: U.S. Department of Education, Planning and Evaluation Service.

Cochran-Smith, M., Albert, L., Dimattia, P., Freedman, S., Jackson, R., Mooney, J., . . . Zollers, N. (1999). Seeking social justice: A teacher education faculty's self-study. *International Journal of Leadership in Education, 2*(3), 229–253.

Coleman, J. S., Campbell, E. Q., Hobson, C. J., McPartland, J., Mood, A. M., Weinfeld, F. D., & York, R. L. (1966). *Equality of educational opportunity.* Washington, DC: Government Printing Office.

Cranton, P. (1992). *Working with adult learners.* Toronto, Canada: Wall & Emerson, Inc.

Crawford, J. (1998). Changes in administrative licensure: 1991–1996. *UCEA Review, 39*(3), 8–10.

Daresh, J. (2002). U.S. school administrator development: Issues and a plan for improvement. In W. Lin (Ed.), *Proceedings on international conference on school leader preparation, licensure/certification, selection, evaluation, and professional development.* Taipei, Taiwan: National Taipei Teachers College.

Delpit, L. (1995). *Other people's children: Cultural conflict in the classroom.* New York, NY: New Press.

Designs for Change (1998). *Practices of schools with substantially improved reading achievement.* Chicago, IL: Chicago Public Schools.

Donmoyer, R. (1999). The continuing quest for a knowledge base: 1976–1998. In J. Murphy & K. Seashore Louis (Eds.), *Handbook of research on educational administration* (pp. 25–43). San Francisco, CA: Jossey-Bass.

Edmonds, R. (1979). Effective schools for the urban poor. *Educational Leadership, 37*(1), 15–24.

Educational Research Service. (1998). *Is there a shortage of qualified candidates for openings in the principalship: An exploratory study.* Arlington, VA: Author.

English, F. (2000). A critical interrogation of Murphy's call for a new center of gravity in educational administration. *Journal of School Leadership, 10*(6), 445–463.

Foster, W. (2004). The decline of the local: A challenge to educational leadership. *Educational Administration Quarterly, 40*(2), 176–191.

Freire, P. (1970/1990). *Pedagogy of the oppressed.* New York, NY: Seabury.

Freire, P. (1973). *Education for critical consciousness.* New York, NY: Continuum.

Fullan, M. (1993). *Change forces: Probing the depths of educational reform.* London, UK: Falmer.

Fullan, M. (1999). *Change forces: The sequel.* Philadelphia, PA: Falmer.

Fullan, M. (2000). *Change forces: The sequel.* London, UK: Falmer.

Fullan, M. (2005). *Leadership & sustainability: Systems thinkers in action.* Thousand Oaks, CA: Sage.

Fullan, M., & Hargreaves, A. (1996). *What's worth fighting for in your school.* New York, NY: Teachers College.

Furman, G. (1998). Postmodernism and community in schools: Unraveling the paradox. *Educational Administration Quarterly, 34*(3), 298–328.

Glickman, C. (2002). *Leadership for learning: How to help teachers succeed.* Alexandria, VA: Association for Supervision and Curriculum Development.

Grogan, M. (Ed.). (2002). Leadership for social justice [Special Issue]. *Journal of School Leadership, 12*(2).

Hale, E., & Moorman, H. (2003). *Preparing school principals: A national perspective on policy and program innovations.* Washington, DC: Institute for Educational Leadership.

Hallinger, P., Bickman, L., & Davis, K. (1996). School context, principal leadership, and student reading achievement. *The Elementary School Journal, 96,* 527–549.

Harlow, J. G. (1962). Purpose-defining: The central function of the school administrator. In J. Culbertson & S. P. Hencley (Eds.), *Preparing administrators: New perspectives* (pp. 61–71). Columbus, OH: University Council for Educational Administration.

Harrison, R., & Hopkins, R. L. (1967). The design of cross-cultural training: An alternative to the university model. *Journal of Applied Behavioral Science, 3*(4), 431–460.

Haycock, K. (2001). Closing the achievement gap. *Educational Leadership, 58*(6), 5–9.

Henze, R., Katz, A., Norte, E., Sather, S., & Walker, E. (2002). *Leading for diversity: How school leaders promote positive interethnic relations.* Thousand Oaks, CA: Corwin.

Jackson, B. (2001). *Exceptional and innovative programs in educational leadership.* A paper commissioned for the First Meeting of the National Commission for the Advancement of Educational Leadership Preparation. Racine, WI.

Jencks, C., & Phillips, M. (1998). *The black-white test score gap.* Washington, DC: Brookings Institution.

Kincheloe, J. L., & Steinberg, S. R. (1995). The more questions we ask, the more questions we ask. In J. L. Kincheloe & S. R. Steinberg (Eds.), *Thirteen questions: Reframing education's conversation* (2nd ed.). New York, NY: Peter Lang.

Ladson-Billings, G. (1994). *The dreamkeepers: Successful teachers of African-American children.* San Francisco, CA: Jossey-Bass.

Larson, C., & Murtadha, K. (2002). Leadership for social justice. In J. Murphy (Ed.), *The educational leadership challenge: Redefining leadership for the 21st century* (pp. 134–161). Chicago, IL: University of Chicago.

Larson, C. L., & Ovando C. J. (2001). *The color of bureaucracy: The politics of equity in multicultural school communities.* Belmont, CA: Wadsworth Thomson Learning.

Lee, V. E., & Smith, J. B. (1994). *Effects of high school restructuring and size on gains in achievement and engagement for early secondary school students.* Madison, WI: University of Wisconsin, Wisconsin Center for School Research, National Center on Effective Secondary Schools.

Lein, L., Johnson, J. F., & Ragland, M. (1997). *Successful Texas schoolwide programs: Research study results.* Austin: Charles A. Dana Center, University of Texas at Austin.

Leithwood, K., Seashore Louis, K., Anderson, S., & Wahlstrom, K. (2004). *How leadership influences student learning.* New York, NY: The Wallace Foundation.

Louis, K. S., & Kruse, S. (1995). *Professionalism and community in schools.* Thousand Oaks, CA: Corwin.

Lyman, L. L., & Villani, C. J. (2002). The complexity of poverty: A missing component of educational leadership programs. *Journal of School Leadership, 12*(3), 246–280.

Marshall, C. (2004). Social justice challenges to educational administration; Introduction to a special issue. *Educational Administration Quarterly, 40*(1), 5–15.

Marzano, R. J. (2003). *What works in schools: Translating research into action.* Alexandria, VA: Association for Supervision and Curriculum Development.

McCarthy, M. (1999). The evolution of educational leadership preparation programs. In J. Murphy & K. Seashore Louis (Eds.), *Handbook of research on educational administration* (pp.119–139). San Francisco, CA: Jossey-Bass.

McCormick, (1987, December). The school executive shortage: How serious is it? *The Education Digest, 55*, 2–5.

Mezirow, J. (1990). *Fostering critical reflection in adulthood: A guide to transformative and emancipatory learning.* San Francisco, CA: Jossey-Bass.

Miron, L. (1996). *Resisting discrimination: Affirmative strategies for principals and teachers.* Thousand Oaks, CA: Corwin.

Moses, R., & Cobb, C. E. (2002). *Radical equations: Math literacy and civil rights.* Boston, MA: Beacon.

Murphy, J. (1999). *The quest for a center: Notes on the state of the profession of educational administration.* Columbia, MO: University Council for Educational Administration.

Murphy, J. (2001, August). *Re-culturing the profession of educational leadership: New blueprints.* Paper commissioned for the first meeting of the National Commission for the Advancement of Educational Leadership Preparation. Racine, WI.

Murphy, J., & Beck, L. (1994). Restructuring the principalship: Challenges and possibilities. In J. Murphy & K. S. Louis (Eds.), *Reshaping the principalship: Insights from transformational reform efforts.* Thousand Oaks, CA: Corwin.

Murtadha-Watts, K. (1999, October). *Negotiating the primacy of culture, race and class with city accountability policy formation.* Paper presented at the annual meeting of the University Council of Educational Administration. Minneapolis, MN.

National Commission on Excellence in Education (1983, April). *A nation at risk: The imperative for educational reform.* Washington, DC: Author.

National Institute on Educational Governance, Finance, Policymaking, and Management (1999). *Effective leaders for today's schools: Synthesis of a policy forum on educational leadership.* Washington, DC: Office of Educational Research and Improvement, U.S. Department of Education.

Newmann, F. M., & Wehlage, G. G. (1995). *Successful school restructuring.* Madison, WI: University of Wisconsin, Wisconsin Center for Educational Research, Center on Organization and Restructuring of Schools.

Noddings, N. (1992). *The challenge to care in schools: Alternative approaches to education.* New York, NY: Teachers College.

Oakes, J., Quartz, K. H., Ryan, S., & Lipton, M. (2000). Becoming good American schools. *Phi Delta Kappan, 81*(8), 568–576.

Odden, A. R., & Odden, E. (1995). *Educational leadership for America's schools.* New York, NY: McGraw-Hill.

Ortiz, A. A. (1997). Learning disabilities occurring concomitantly with linguistic differences. *Journal of Learning Disabilities, 30*(3), 321–332.

Petersen, K. (1982). Making sense of principals' work. *The Australian Administrator, 3*(3), 1–4.

Puma, M. J., Karweit, N., Price, C., Ricciuiti, A., Thompson, W., & Vaden-Kiernan, M. (1997). *Prospects: Final report on student outcomes.* Washington, DC: U.S. Department of Education, Planning and Evaluation Services.

Purpel, D. (1989). *The moral & spiritual crisis in education: A curriculum for justice & compassion in education.* New York, NY: Bergin & Garvey.

Rapp, D. (2002). Social justice and the importance of rebellious imaginations. *Journal of School Leadership, 12*(3), 226–245.

Ridenour, C. S., First, P. F., Lydon, A., & Partlow, M. C. (2001). Issues of racial, ethnic, and gender diversity in preparing school administrators. In T. J. Kowalski (Ed.), *21st century challenges for school administrators* (pp. 146–164). Lanham, MD: Scarecrow.

Riester, A. F., Pursch, V., & Skrla L. (2002). Principals for social justice: Leaders of school success for children from low-income homes. *Journal of School Leadership, 12*(3), 281–304.

Rokeach, M. (1960). *The open and closed mind: Investigation into the nature of belief systems and personality systems.* New York, NY: Basic Books, Inc.

Rosenholtz, S. J. (1985). Effective schools: Interpreting the evidence. *American Journal of Education, 93*(3), 352–388.

Rusch, E. A. (2004). Gender and race in leadership preparation: A constrained discourse. *Educational Administration Quarterly, 40*(1), 16–48.

Scheurich, J. J. (1998). Highly successful and loving, public elementary schools populated mainly by low-ses children of color: Core beliefs and cultural characteristics. *Urban Education, 33*(4), 451–491.

Scheurich, J. J., & Laible, J. (1999). The buck stops here—in our preparation programs: Educational leadership for all children (no exceptions allowed). *Educational Administration Quarterly, 31*(2), 313–322.

Scheurich, J., & Skrla, L. (2003). *Leadership for equity and excellence: Creating high achievement classrooms, schools, and districts.* Thousand Oaks, CA: Corwin.

Schon, D. (1987). *Educating the reflective practitioner.* San Francisco, CA: Jossey-Bass.

Senge, P. (1990). *The fifth discipline: The art & practice of the learning organization.* New York, NY: Doubleday.

Shapiro, J., & Stefkovich, J. (2001). *Ethical leadership and decision making in education: Applying theoretical perspectives to complex dilemmas.* Mahwah, NJ: Lawrence Erlbaum Associates.

Shields, C., Larocque, L., & Oberg, S. (2002). A dialogue about race and ethnicity in education: Struggling to understand issues in cross-cultural leadership. *Journal of School Leadership, 12*(2), 116–137.

Shields, C., & Oberg, S. (2000). *Year-round schooling: Promises and pitfalls.* Lanham, MD: Scarecrow/Technomics.

Shields, C., & Seltzer, P. (1997). Complexities and paradoxes of community: Toward a more useful conceptualization of community. *Educational Administration Quarterly, 33*(4), 413–439.

Shouse, R. C. (1996). Academic press and sense of community: Conflict, congruence, and implications for student achievement. *Social Psychology of Education, 1*(1), 47–68.

Skrla, L., Scheurich, J. J., Johnson, J. F., & Koschoreck, J. W. (2001). Accountability for equity: Can state policy leverage social justice? *International Journal of Leadership in Education, 4*(3), 237–260.

Solomon, R. P. (2002). School leaders and antiracism: Overcoming pedagogical and political obstacles. *Journal of School Leadership, 12*(2), 174–197.

Starratt, R. J. (2003). Democratic leadership theory in late modernity: An oxymoron or ironic possibility? In P. Begley (Ed.), *The ethical dimensions of school leadership* (pp. 13–31). Boston, MA: Kluwer.

Taylor, B. M., Pearson, P. D., Clark, K., & Walpole, S. (2000). Effective schools and accomplished teachers: Lessons about primary-grade reading instruction in low-income schools. *Elementary School Journal, 101,* 121–166.

Taylor, B. M., Pressley, M., & Pearson, P. D. (2002). Research-supported characteristics of teachers and schools that promote reading achievement. In P. D. Pearson & B. M. Taylor (Eds.), *Teaching reading: Effective schools, accomplished teachers* (pp. 361–373). Mahwah, NJ: Erlbaum.

Teske, P., & Schneider, M. (1999). *The importance of leadership: The role of school principals.* Arlington, VA: The PricewaterhouseCoopers Endowment for the Business of Government.

Valenzuela, A. (1999). *Subtractive schooling: US-Mexican youth and the politics of caring.* Albany NY: State University of New York.

Waters, T., & Grubb, S. (2004). *The leadership we need: Using research to strengthen the use of standards for administrator preparation and licensure program.* Aurora, CO: Mid-continent Research for Education and Learning.

Chapter 2

Transformative Andragogical Theory and Practice

INTRODUCTION

Transformative learning is a process of experiential learning, critical self-reflection, and rationale discourse that can be stimulated by people, events, or changes in context, which challenge the learner's basic assumptions of the world. Transformative learning leads to a new way of seeing. "Values are not necessarily changed, but are examined—their source is identified, and they are accepted and justified or revised or possibly rejected" (Cranton, 1992, p. 146).

Transformative andragogy is the art and science of helping others learn. As such, the three interwoven theoretical perspectives of adult learning theory (Knowles, 1984), transformative learning theory (Mezirow, 2000), and critical social theory (Freire, 1970) are relevant to the reform of principal preparation programs. Since future leaders are adults who bring a wealth of knowledge and experience with them, preparation programs can help them build on that foundation through participation in transformative learning strategies (see chapters 4, 5, and 6 for complete description).

Learning is enhanced when curriculum and instruction integrate student experiences with the development of meaning. Iran-Nejad, McKeachie, and Berliner (1990) agree, noting that "the more meaningful, the more deeply or elaboratively processed, the more situated in context, and the more rooted in cultural, background, metacognitive, and personal . . . the more readily it is understood, learned, and remembered" (p. 511). Together, the andragogical processes of critical reflection (Brookfield, 1995), rational discourse (Mezirow, 1991), and policy praxis (Freire, 1985) can lead to a transformation of one's personal agency, as well as deepen one's sense of social responsibility toward and with others (see figure A).

This chapter describes the theoretical foundation supporting this transformative andragogical model and then reports findings from a research study aimed at documenting theory into practice applications. The question to be answered is not whether the andragogical strategies lead to verifiable and enduring transformation either for individual principals or on a larger scale. But rather, through participation in such activities, do some future and current leaders develop their own critical, self-reflexive pedagogies and andragogies for their school communities that invite, rather than repress or deny, differences and diversity and action for justice and equity?

ADULT LEARNING THEORY

Adult learning is probably the most studied topic in adult education. The learner, the learning process, and the context of learning form the cornerstone of the field of adult education. Adult education takes place in a wide variety of situations (including principal preparation programs) and involves a set of activities or experiences engaged in by adults that lead to changes in thinking, values, and behavior. Knowles (1984), one of the most influential figures in the field of adult education, is best known for his work on the factors that distinguish pedagogy from andragogy. Although his assertions and claims of difference are the subject of considerable debate (see Davenport, 1993; Jarvis, 1987; Tennant, 1996), Knowles defined pedagogy as the art and science of teaching and andragogy as the art and science of helping others to learn. According to Confessore (1999), andragogical perspectives, processes, and strategies are essential components for preparation programs.

> One of the biggest challenges facing the faculty member of the future will be coaching learners to develop the capacity to form opinions independently and clarify beliefs. Of all the goals necessary for independent learners, this is the most important. Information, no matter how accessible, is useless—and perhaps even dangerous—without the sagacity to understand one's own belief structure and the capacity to develop well-formed and substantial opinion. (p. 165)

For Knowles, andragogy was premised on at least four crucial assumptions about the characteristics of adult learners that are different from the assumptions about child learners. A fifth assumption was added later.

1. *Self-concept*: As a person matures, his self-concept moves from one of being a dependent personality toward one of being a self-directed human being.

2. *Experience*: As a person matures, he accumulates a growing reservoir of experience that becomes an increasing resource for learning.
3. *Readiness to learn*: As a person matures, his readiness to learn becomes oriented increasingly to the developmental tasks of his social roles.
4. *Orientation to learning*: As a person matures, his time perspective changes from one of postponed application of knowledge to immediacy of application, and accordingly his orientation toward learning shifts from one of subject-centeredness to one of problem-centeredness.
5. *Motivation to learn*: As a person matures, the motivation to learn is internal. (Knowles, 1984, p. 12)

Despite ongoing internal debates, misconceptions, and a lack of universal agreement, the following four major research areas constitute an espoused theory of adult learning that informs our preparation of future educational leaders: (1) self-directed learning, (2) critical reflection, (3) experiential learning, and (4) learning to learn (Brookfield, 1995). The first adult learning theory construct, *self-directed learning*, focuses on the process by which adults take control of their own learning, set their own goals, locate appropriate resources, decide on which methods to use, and evaluate their progress (see Candy, 1991; Field, 1991; and Knowles, 1975). The notion of self-directed learning has evolved over time. It is described as a goal, a process, and a learner characteristic that changes with the nature of the learning (Jarvis, 1992). In clarifying the complexity of self-direction, Candy (1991) referred to four distinct (but related) phenomena:

"Self-direction" as a personal attribute (personal autonomy); "self-direction" as the willingness and capacity to conduct one's own education (self-management); "self-direction" as a mode of organizing instruction in formal settings (learner-control); and "self-direction" as the individual noninstitutional pursuit of learning opportunities in the "natural society setting" (autodidaxy). (p. 23)

The second adult learning theory construct, *thinking contextually and critically*, is embedded within the realm of developmental psychology and the constructs of logic, dialectical thinking, working intelligence, reflective judgment, postformal reasoning, and epistemic cognition (Brookfield, 1991). The ideas of critical theory—particularly that of ideological critique—are central to critical reflection. To the contemporary educational critic Giroux (1983), "the ideological dimension that underlies all critical reflection is that it lays bare the historically and socially sedimented values at work in the construction of knowledge, social relations, and material practices . . . it situates critique within a radical notion of interest and social transformation" (pp. 154–155).

An important element in this tradition is the thought of Gramsci (1978), whose concept of hegemony explains the way in which people are convinced to embrace dominant ideologies as always being in their own best interests. According to Mezirow (1985), critical reflection is an "understanding of the historical, cultural, and biographical reasons for one's needs, wants and interests . . . such self-knowledge is a prerequisite for autonomy in self-directed learning" (p. 27).

Central to the concept of andragogy is the third construct, *experiential learning* (Jarvis, 1987; Kolb, 1984). As the founding parent of experiential learning, Dewey (1938) claimed that not only experiences are the key building blocks of learning but also action is an intrinsic part of the learning cycle; this implies learning by doing, as well as a practical understanding of the world.

Building on the work of Dewey (1916, 1938) and Piaget (1968), Kolb (1984) viewed experiential learning as basically a mechanism by which individuals structured reality. It encompassed four steps: (1) concrete experience, (2) reflective observation, (3) abstract conceptualization, and (4) active experimentation. Two underlying axes structured the four capacities or modes of adapting to the world, leading to Kolb's four different sectors of knowledge and corresponding learning styles: (1) convergence, (2) divergence, (3) assimilation, and (4) accommodation.

The ability to become skilled at learning in a range of different situations and through a range of different styles is the fourth founding construct of adult learning theory. According to Kitchener and King (1990), the fourth construct, *learning to learn*, involves an epistemological awareness. It means that adults possess a self-conscious awareness of how it is they come to know what they know—an awareness of the reasoning, assumptions, evidence, and justifications that underlie our beliefs that something is true.

Developmental theorists usually portray individuals as moving from a black-and-white (true vs. false) perception of the world to a relativistic perception of it. At the earlier stages, reflective thinking or questioning of assumptions does not occur. At the other end of the continuum, the individual whose reflective judgment is developed perceives knowledge to be the product of inquiry and reflection. The process of inquiry is seen to be, in itself, fallible; justification is based on a rational evaluation of the evidence. The epistemic assumptions of Kitchener's (1983) seven stages included:

- Beliefs need no justification; what is believed is true.
- Knowledge is absolutely certain but may not be immediately available.
- Knowledge is absolutely certain or temporarily uncertain.
- Knowledge is idiosyncratic; some information may be in error or lost, therefore one cannot know with certainty.
- Knowledge is contextual and subjective; it is available through interpretation.
- Knowledge is constructed by each person and is based on the evaluation of evidence and argument.
- Knowledge is the product of rational inquiry, which is fallible.

Mezirow (1991) moved "beyond andragogy" and proposed a theory of transformative learning "that can explain how adult learners make sense or meaning of their experiences, the nature of the structures that influence the way they construe experience, the dynamics involved in modifying meanings, and the way the structures of meanings themselves undergo changes when learners find them to be dysfunctional" (p. xii).

Mezirow (1990) defined it as a process of reflection and action. "From this vantage point, adult education becomes the process of assisting those who are fulfilling adult roles to understand the meaning of their experience by participating more fully and freely in rational discourse to validate expressed ideas and to take action upon the resulting insights. . . . Rational thought and action are the cardinal goals of adult education" (p. 354) This process of reflection and action is crucial to preparing future leaders who can and will leverage small changes in daily practice that begin to transform bigger systems.

TRANSFORMATIVE LEARNING THEORY

Transformative learning changes the way people see themselves and their world. It attempts to explain how their expectations, framed within cultural assumptions and presuppositions, directly influence the meaning they derive from their experiences. Relying heavily on adult learning theory and Habermas's (1984) communicative theory, Mezirow (1991) proposed a theory of transformative learning that can explain the following:

> how adult learners make sense or meaning of their experiences, the nature of the structures that influence the way they construe experience, the dynamics involved in modifying meanings, and the way the structures of meanings themselves undergo changes when learners find them to be dysfunctional. (p. xii)

Three themes of Mezirow's transformative theory are (1) the centrality of experience, (2) critical reflection, and (3) rational discourse (see also Boyd, 1991; Cranton, 1994; Kegan, 1994). Perspective transformation explains how the meaning structures that adults have acquired over a lifetime become transformed. These meaning structures, which are inclusive of meaning schemes and meaning perspectives, are frames of reference that are based on the totality of individuals' cultural and contextual experiences. Meaning schemes, the smaller components, are "made up of specific knowledge, beliefs, value judgments, and feelings that constitute interpretations of experience" (Mezirow, 1991, pp. 5–6). For learners to change their "meaning schemes," they must engage in critical reflection of their experiences, which in turn leads to a perspective transformation.

The purposes of critical reflection are to externalize and investigate power relationships and to uncover hegemonic assumptions. Critical reflection, according to Brookfield (1995), focuses on three interrelated processes:

(1) the process by which adults question and then replace or reframe an assumption that up to that point has been uncritically accepted as representing commonsense wisdom;

(2) the process through which adults take alternative perspectives on previously taken-for-granted ideas, actions, forms of reasoning, and ideologies; and

(3) the process by which adults come to recognize the hegemonic aspects of dominant cultural values. (p. 2)

Mezirow (1998) posited that adult learning occurs in four ways— (1) elaborating existing frames of reference, (2) learning frames of references, (3) transforming points of view, and (4) transforming habits of mind—and named critical reflection as a component of all four. Mezirow argued that the overall purpose of adult development is to realize one's agency through increasingly expanding awareness and critical reflection. Within the context of preparation programs, the educational tasks of critical reflection involve helping future leaders become aware of oppressive structures and practices, developing tactical awareness of how they might change these, and building the confidence and ability to work for collective change.

According to transformative learning theory (Mezirow, 1991), rational discourse is a means for testing the validity of one's construction of meaning. It is the essential medium through which transformation is promoted and developed. Rational discourse involves a commitment to extended and repeated conversations that evolve over time into a culture of careful listening and cautious openness to new perspectives, not shared understanding in the sense of consensus, but rather deeper and richer understandings of our own biases as well as where our colleagues are coming from on particular issues and how each of us differently constructs those issues.

As such, participation in extended and repeated discourse about social justice, equity, and excellence can provide unique opportunities for future leaders' growth, transformation, and empowerment and can increase their understanding of how issues of race and ethnicity affect the educational experiences for all students. To do this, Shields, Larocque, and Oberg (2002) advocate for the following:

> As we struggle to understand how issues of race and ethnicity affect the educational experiences for all students, we must work to overcome our prejudices by listening carefully to those whose backgrounds, perspectives, and understandings differ from our own. We must examine popular assumptions as well as

the politically correct stereotypes that educators often use to explain what is happening in today's multicultural society and its increasingly ethnically heterogeneous schools. Engaging in socially just leadership requires us to maintain an open conversation, to examine and reexamine our perceptions and those of others, constantly looking beneath the surface and seeking alternative explanations and ways of understanding. (p. 134)

Engaging in the critical self-reflection that may lead to changes in perspective is, in itself, a process that requires self-awareness, planning, skill, support, and discourse with others. Participation in rational discourse is also part of the process of learner empowerment. Mezirow (1996) outlined seven ideal conditions for rational discourse:

1. Have accurate and complete information.
2. Be free from coercion and distorting self-conception.
3. Be able to weigh evidence and assess arguments objectively.
4. Be open to alternative perspectives.
5. Be able to reflect critically on presuppositions and their consequences.
6. Have equal opportunity to participate (including the chance to challenge, question, refute, and reflect, and to hear others do the same).
7. Be able to accept an informed, objective, and rational consensus as a legitimate test of validity. (p. 78)

CRITICAL SOCIAL THEORY

Freire's (1970) work portrayed a practical and theoretical approach to emancipation through education. He wanted people to develop an "ontological vocation" (p. 12), a theory of existence that views people as subjects, not objects, who are constantly reflecting and acting on the transformation of their world so it can become a more equitable place for all to live.

Unlike Mezirow's personal transformation, Freire was much more concerned about a social transformation, a demythologizing of reality and an awakening of critical consciousness whereby people perceive the social, political, and economic contradictions of their time and take action against the oppressive elements. "Like Mezirow, Freire sees critical reflection as central to transformation in context to problem-posing and dialogue with other learners. However, in contrast, Freire sees its purpose based on a rediscovery of power such that the more critically aware learners become the more they are able to transform society and subsequently their own reality" (Taylor, 1998, p. 17).

Though somewhat rudimentary, Freire (1970) offers a basic sociohistorical three-stage model of individual development culminating in dialectical thought. At one extreme of the continuum is found the relatively "intransitive" consciousness that lives passively within a given reality, and at the other, is the active "transitive" consciousness that engages the world cognitively and politically.

> The critically transitive consciousness is characterized by depth in the interpretation of problems; by the substitution of casual principles for magical explanations; by the testing of one's "findings" and by openness to revisions; by the attempt to avoid distortion when perceiving problems and to avoid preconceived notions when analyzing them; by refusing to transfer responsibility; by rejecting passive positions; by soundness of argumentation; by the practice of dialogue rather than polemics, by receptivity to the new for reasons beyond mere novelty and by the good sense not to reject the old just because it is old—by accepting what is valid on both old and new. (Freire, 1973, p. 18)

Freire's process of developing *conscientization* means that, through dialogue, future leaders can begin to understand themselves as active agents, enabling them to identify and create conditions for the possibility of change in oppressive sociopolitical constructs. Performing as critically thinking and speaking subjects in the classroom provides, for adult learners, the basis for performing as citizen-critics outside it, as well (Giroux, 1992).

Freire's notion of dialogue isn't just about deepening understanding, it is about respect and giving future leaders an opportunity to rehearse social criticism and actually engage in sociocultural issues. The purpose of a dialogic relationship, according to Freire (1993), is "to stimulate doubt, criticism, curiosity, questioning, a taste for risk-taking, the adventure of creating" (p. 50). It is "the moment when humans meet to reflect on their reality as they make and remake it" (Shor & Freire, 1987, p. 112). Dialogue leads us to act in ways that make for justice and human flourishing.

Building on these Freirean interpretations of praxis, reflection becomes truly critical only when it leads to some form of transformative social action. hooks (1994) commended Freire's (1970) commitment to counteract the "false consciousness" prevalent in members of marginalized groups and identified the real dilemma in education as one of striking a balance between empowering and equipping students for what makes for success in the "world" (see also Delpit, 1995).

hooks's *Teaching to Transgress: Education as the Practice of Freedom* (1994) echoed Freire's philosophy and highlighted the importance of an educational system that counteracts the propagation of ideological elements in a racist, sexist, and classist society by interrogating the political implications of "externally" imposed curriculum standards, "banking" pedagogical approaches, and "hierarchical" arrangements within educational settings.

Critical social theory calls educators to activism. Activists stand between the constituent base and the powerholders. Their role is to organize constituents, articulate their concerns, and negotiate/advocate on their behalf with pow-erholders to develop a repertoire of action strategies with the long-term aim of shifting power (Tilley, 1993). Educational activists recognize the ethical dimensions of teaching other people's children, they work to provide other people's children with the highest quality of education they would desire for their own children, and they learn to work as an ally with the community.

Educational activists share power with marginalized groups, they seek out networks, and they teach others to act politically and to advocate individu-ally and collectively for themselves and other marginalized groups. Activism requires a "critical consciousness" and an ability to organize "reflectively for action rather than for passivity" (Freire, 1985, p. 82). Banks (1981) concurred:

> They must also develop a sense of political efficacy, and be given practice in social action strategies which teaches them how to get power without violence and further exclusion. . . . Opportunities for social action, in which students have experience in obtaining and exercising power, should be emphasized within a curriculum that is designed to help liberate excluded ethnic groups. (p. 149)

Social justice activists espouse a theory of social critique, embrace a greater sense of civic duty, and willingly become active agents for political and social change. They are committed to an agenda in which past practices, anchored in open and residual racism, gender exclusivity, homophobia, class discrimination, and religious intolerance, are confronted and changed over time. They challenge exclusion, isolation, and marginalization of the stranger; respond to oppression with courage; empower the powerless; and transform existing social inequalities and injustices.

Educational leaders committed to equity understand and create oppor-tunities for learning for all students by dealing with issues of context and achievement. Socioeconomic and political discrepancies in the larger social order are analyzed in relationship to school routines, procedures, curriculum and textbook adoption, and classroom pedagogies. Leaders for social justice examine power relations within schools and society, scrutinize differential schooling, and critique social class stratifications. The framework imple-mented and evaluated in this book was designed in an effort to prepare such leaders—leaders attuned to the complexities of changing demographics, leaders willing and able "to engage in and facilitate critical and constructive inquiry" (Sirontnik & Kimball, 1996, p. 187).

PRAXIS

Praxis is an old and much-used philosophical term employed by nearly every major Western philosopher including Aristotle, Bacon, Kant, Hegel, and Marx. Because of its long history, praxis has a variety of possible definitions, almost all of which describe a relationship between theory and practice. While some of these definitions range from a complete separation between theory and practice to a complete conflation of the two, modern philosophers tend to favor a definition that highlights the interdependence of thought and action. In fact, within the past twenty years, contemporary educators have embraced the term *praxis*, using it to mean reflective practice or a union between thought and action.

Proponents of praxis believe that theory should be grounded in practice in order to keep theory applicable, pragmatic, and meaningful. As such *praxis* refers to the process by which a theory or lesson becomes part of a lived experience. Rather than a lesson being simply absorbed at the intellectual level, ideas are tested and experienced in the real world, followed by an opportunity for reflective contemplation. In this way, abstract concepts are connected with lived reality. The *American Heritage Dictionary* defines praxis as "practical application or exercise of a branch of learning."

For Aristotle, praxis is guided by a moral disposition to act truly and rightly, a concern to further human well-being and good life. For Aristotle, *praxis* meant reflective action informed by *phronesis*, the prudential reasoning and practical skill that enables a person to transform a tradition's meaning into the immediate social context. In praxis there can be no prior knowledge of the right means by which one realizes the end in a particular situation. For the end itself is only specified in deliberating about the means appropriate to a particular situation.

The way to achieve something depends on what one wants to achieve, and vice versa. There is a continual interplay between ends and means. This process involves interpretation, understanding, and application in "one unified process." Praxis is not simply action based on reflection. It is action that embodies certain qualities. These include a commitment to human well-being and the search for truth, and respect for others. It is the action of people who are free, who are able to act for themselves.

Moreover, praxis is always risky. It is about both production and "right conduct." It is informed action, as well as politically and ethically conscious action that in its functioning overlaps practical and productive knowledge. According to Carr and Kemmis (1986), it requires that a person "make a wise and prudent practical judgment about how to act in *this* situation" (p. 32).

As such, word and action, action and reflection, and theory and practice are all facets of the same idea. This action is not merely the doing of something, what Aristotle described as *poiesis*, and Freire later referred to as *activism*. *Poiesis* is about acting upon, doing to: it is about working with objects. Praxis, however, is creative: it is other-seeking and dialogic. Praxis seeks to get at the interaction of deed and thought, the holistic embodiment of meaning. It is correctly understood as the critical relationship between theory and practice whereby each is dialectically influenced and transformed by the other.

More technical, philosophically grounded definitions of praxis describe it as an act in opposition to meaningless, uncreative labor; sometimes it is defined in opposition to abstract, inert theory. One of the latest definitions includes one by Hegel, who placed the practical above the theoretical and also thought that their unity must be found in a third, higher moment. For Hegel, the practical comes first. The power of Marx's critique of Hegel is that it attempts to more strongly ground a theory of the social subject and mutual recognition in a theory of domination—in the oppressive historical contingencies and structures of economic and social life. In Marxist theory, *praxis* means the imperative to apply what you learn to change what you observe; to put theory into action.

The particular focus of Marx is on capitalist societies where the commodification of labor results in "alienated" labor. According to this model, only the worker as "slave" is in a position to understand true freedom as equality; the resulting revolutionary consciousness then becomes the basis of a new form of society that abolishes class division. How does the working class become self-conscious and create a revolution? How does the culturally deprived, alienated worker become an active learner when these very conditions inhibit the formation of reflective consciousness? According to Marx, revolutionary praxis is an activity that implies a theory of learning: the process through which dominated consciousness might be transformed into emancipatory consciousness.

Marx's theory of action takes the form of a "productive paradigm" that views praxis as a form of productive activity (work) understood in terms of a subject-object relation. According to Habermas, however, the model of praxis as production tends to equate action with work (instrumental action), thus downplaying the linguistic and communicative aspects of social life. For Habermas and Freire, the key to reconstructing the theory of praxis is found in the dialogical learning processes that might mediate between the realities of human need and the capacity to reflect and act in liberating ways.

From this perspective, Freire extends the Aristotelian concept of praxis as ethics in practice. His concept of praxis is based on the analysis of the simplest element of human dialogue, the word. Freire explains that the word is two-dimensional, comprised of reflection and action. He contends that these two dimensions are in such radical interaction that if one is sacrificed—even in part—the other immediately suffers. According to Freire, "there is no true word that is not at the same time a praxis."

Freire's (1970) account of praxis is based on the richly textured synthetic vision of the "pedagogy of the oppressed." Freire's liberation pedagogy is a cultural action or process toward liberation. It has two phases: (1) critical consciousness (conscientization) and (2) critical praxis. Conscientization is the process by which a group (class) of people become aware of their cultural oppression, of their "colonized mentality," and, as a result, discover that they have a popular culture, a political identity, and a societal role.

Conscientization is in itself a liberatory process, as one is freed from self-deprecation. It is important for Freire that the oppressors must also be considered, as they too must become aware of their dehumanizing situation, which maintains injustice. But consciousness alone is not sufficient. Conscientization requires critical praxis as a second phase. Such praxis is not a revolutionary seizure of power from the oppressors. Rather, it is a peaceful intervention in order to develop alternatives. Developing such alternatives must include the oppressors, by transforming unjust power relations through dialogue. According to Freire (1970), praxis is the dialectical union of reflection and action; praxis is at the heart of human nature since human activity consists of action and reflection: it is praxis; it is transformation of the world. And as praxis it requires theory to illuminate it.

Praxis is an active learning experience. It is the act of reflectively constructing or reconstructing the social world. It is a dynamic process that recognizes the reciprocal relationship between theory and practice and how each can inform the other. Praxis is thoughtful action—the kind of action that unites the elements of intention, mindfulness, and critical theory. This is distinguished from the task-oriented "doing."

Praxis refers to a relationship between theory and practice in which one creates/constructs knowledge and meaning from his or her experiences. Within a praxis framework, one assesses a situation, understands it through reflection and discussions, and makes sound judgments that lead to justifiable actions. One is then able to perceive situations within the larger context, make generalizations from his or her experiences, and take action as a responsible professional to modify/develop all levels of practice.

Praxis is reflective of a relationship between individuals and their wider community. It means bridging the gap between individual and fragmented awareness on the one hand and building sustainable communities as alternatives on the other. What is fundamental to the concept of praxis is that it is the integration of reflection with action, or simply, it is action informed by theory, with a view to transformation of the larger social community. The nature of this interaction may be that theory transforms action, which may in turn reshape theory, and so on, in a holistic relationship. It is also essential to this concept that the individuals and/or community are empowered to decide on the changes best suited to their specific contexts and are enabled to identify or develop the tools to effect such change.

For educators, praxis is the continual process of connecting educational theory to practice and practice to educational theory with the goal of improving each. *Praxis occurs when theory and practice are connected, that is, when theory informs practice and practice brings theory to fruition logically and responsibly.* Engaging in praxis creates a cyclical pattern of research followed by practice, then evaluation—leading back to theory, which may be confirmed, refined, or reformulated. The pattern validates educational claims and improves day-to-day practice. Praxis empowers future leaders to ask questions central to teaching and learning in the contemporary world, creating a network of shared knowledge and answers we can all use. From a foundation of individual experience, one builds universal possibilities capable of transforming the aim of education from knowledge to action.

CONCLUSION

Pounder, Reitzug, and Young (2002) noted that leaders must be provided with new analytical skills, knowledge, and dispositions to promote social justice in schools. Among their recommendations they suggested a range of ideas: participating in field-based inquiry focused on oppression and discrimination, analyzing empirical data regarding racism in schools, examining stereotypes related to oppression, facilitating the creation of a rigorous and inclusive curriculum, and developing socially just practices among all individuals within the school community.

When both discourse and practice consistently, explicitly, and critically interrogate the historical and present-day intersections of race, culture, gender, and foster a self-reflexive engagement with difference, educators can open up more meaningful, situated ways of knowing self and other and rethinking extant relations of power (Asher & Crocco, 2001). The next three chapters highlight some of the more possible effects of the andragogical processes used. In chapter 4, the impact of critical reflection is explored through future leaders' reported growth in awareness of self. In chapter 5, Mezirow's notion of rational discourse is considered through adult learners' described active engagement with, and acknowledgment of, others. And in chapter 6, to a lesser degree, the importance of Freire's praxis is reiterated and then examined through adult learners' dialogue and expressed desire, commitment, and in some cases, actual ability to take action and advocate for change.

CRITICAL QUESTIONS

1. Does your school, district, or state use the tenets of adult learning theory when planning and implementing professional development plans? Why/ why not? How might transformative learning theory and critical social theory be incorporated into those plans?

2. *What realistic strategies can a principal use to help his or her faculty and staff recognize and examine differences in terms of the context-specific intersections of race, class, gender, sexuality, culture, and language of his or her students?*

3. *How might a principal define and really use praxis with his or her faculty? Is it possible? Find and describe one concrete example whereby a new educational concept was first introduced and explained at the intellectual level, and then ideas were tested and experienced in the real world, followed by an opportunity for reflective contemplation. What was the result? Why?*

REFERENCES

Asher, N., & Crocco, M. S. (2001). (En)gendering multicultural identities and representations. *Theory and Research in Social Education, 29*(1), 129–151.

Banks, J. (1981). *Multiethnic education: Theory and practice.* Boston, MA: Allyn & Bacon.

Boyd, R. D. (1991). *Personal transformations in small groups.* New York, NY: Routledge.

Brookfield, S. D. (1991). The development of critical reflection in adulthood. *New Education, 13*(1), 39–48.

Brookfield, S. D. (1995). *Becoming a critically reflective teacher.* San Francisco, CA: Jossey-Bass.

Candy, P. C. (1991). *Self-direction for lifelong learning.* San Francisco, CA: Jossey-Bass.

Carr, W., & Kemmis, S. (1986). *Becoming critical. Education, knowledge and action research.* Lewes, UK: Falmer.

Confessore, S. J. (1999). New learning approaches: Conceptualizing the learning—teaching interaction. In V. Bianco-Mathis & N. Chaloksky (Eds.), *The full-time faculty handbook.* Thousand Oaks, CA: SAGE Publications.

Cranton, P. (1992). *Working with adult learners.* Toronto, Canada: Wall & Emerson.

Cranton, P. (1994). *Understanding and promoting transformative learning: A guide for educators of adults.* San Francisco, CA: Jossey-Bass.

Davenport, J. (1993). Is there any way out of the andragogy mess? In M. Thorpe, R. Edwards & A. Hanson (Eds.), *Culture and processes of adult learning.* London, UK: Routledge.

Delpit, L. (1995). *Other people's children: Cultural conflict in the classroom.* New York, NY: New Press.

Dewey, J. (1916). *Democracy and education: An introduction to the philosophy of education.* New York, NY: Macmillan.

Dewey, J. (1938). *Experience and education.* New York, NY: Simon and Schuster.

Dunn, J. M. (1987). Personal beliefs and public policy. In F. S. Bolin & J. M. Falk (Eds.), *Teacher renewal: Professional issues, personal choices* (pp. 76–86). New York, NY: Teachers College.

Field, L. (1991). Guglielmino's self-directed learning readiness scale: Should it continue to be used? *Adult Education Quarterly, 41,* 100–103.

Freire, P. (1970/1992). *Pedagogy of the oppressed.* New York, NY: Seabury.

Freire, P. (1973). *Education for critical consciousness.* New York, NY: Continuum.

Freire, P. (1985). *The politics of education.* New York, NY: Seabury.

Freire, P. (1993). *Pedagogy of the city.* New York, NY: Continuum.

Giroux, H. (1983). *Theory and resistance in education: A pedagogy for the opposition.* Westport, CN: Bergin and Garvey.

Giroux, H. (1992). *Border crossings: Cultural workers and the politics of education.* New York, NY: Routledge.

Gramsci, A. (1978). *Selections from the prison notebooks.* London, UK: Lawrence and Wishart.

Habermas, J. (1984). *The theory of communicative action. Vol. 1: Reason and the rationalization of society* (T. McCarthy, trans.). Boston, MA: Beacon.

hooks, b. (1994). *Teaching to transgress: Education as the practice of freedom.* New York, NY: Routledge.

Iran-Nejad, A., McKeachie, W. J., & Berliner, D. C. (1990). The multisource nature of learning: An introduction. *Review of Educational Research, 60*(4), 509–515.

Jarvis, P. (1987). *Adult learning in the social context.* London, UK: Croom Helm.

Jarvis, P. (1992). *Paradoxes of learning: On becoming an individual in society.* San Francisco, CA: Jossey-Bass.

Kegan, R. (1994). *In over our heads.* Cambridge. MA: Harvard University.

Kitchener, K. S. (1983). Cognition, metacognition and epistemic cognition. *Human Development, 26,* 222–223.

Kitchener, K. S., & King, P. M. (1990). The reflective judgment model: Transforming assumptions about knowing. In J. Mezirow (Ed.), *Fostering critical reflection in adulthood* (pp. 159–176). San Francisco, CA: Jossey-Bass.

Knowles, M. (1975). *Self-directed learning.* New York, NY: Association Press.

Knowles, M. (1984). *The adult learner: A neglected species* (3rd ed.). Houston, TX: Gulf Publishing.

Kolb, D. A. (1984). *Experiential learning.* Englewood Cliffs, NJ: Prentice-Hall.

Mezirow, J. (1985). A critical theory of self-directed learning. In S. Brookfield (Ed.), *Self-directed learning from theory to practice. New directions for continuing education* (pp. 17–30). San Francisco, CA: Jossey-Bass.

Mezirow, J. (1990). *Fostering critical reflection in adulthood: A guide to transformative and emancipatory learning.* San Francisco, CA: Jossey-Bass.

Mezirow, J. (1991). *Transformative dimensions of adult learning.* San Francisco, CA: Jossey-Bass.

Mezirow, J. (1996). Contemporary paradigms of learning. *Adult Education Quarterly, 46,* 158–172.

Mezirow, J. (1998). On critical reflection. *Adult Education Quarterly, 48*(3), 185–198.

Mezirow, J. (2000). *Learning as transformation: Critical perspectives on a theory in progress.* San Francisco, CA: Jossey-Bass.

Piaget, J. (1968). *Six psychological studies.* London, UK: University of London.

Pounder, D., Reitzug, U., & Young, M. (2002). Preparing school leaders for school improvement, social justice, and community. In J. Murphy (Ed.), *The educational leadership challenge: Redefining leadership for the 21st century* (pp. 261–288). Chicago, IL: University of Chicago.

Shields, C., Larocque, L., & Oberg, S. (2002). A dialogue about race and ethnicity in education: Struggling to understand issues in cross-cultural leadership. *Journal of School Leadership, 12*(2), 116–137.

Shor, I., & Freire, P. (1987). What is the "dialogical method" of teaching? *Journal of Education, 169*(3), 110–117.

Sirontnik, K., & Kimball, K. (1996). Preparing educators for leadership: In praise of experience. *Journal of School Leadership, 6*(2), 180–201.

Taylor, E. W. (1998). *The theory and practice of transformative learning: A critical review*. ERIC Clearinghouse on Adult, Career, and Vocational Education. Columbus, OH.

Tennant, M. (1996). *Psychology and adult learning*. London, UK: Routledge.

Tilley, C. (1993). Social movements as historically specific clusters of political performances. *Berkley Journal of Sociology, 38*, 1–30.

Chapter 3

Recent Research for Section I

INTRODUCTION

This chapter was written for the second edition of this book, and it reviews the literature about "Section I: Transformative Ideas and the Contextual Background," which was published during the years following the publication of the first edition. Initially presenting findings regarding school leaders' great influence on student learning, this chapter examines how school leaders can utilize this significant influence to ensure that all students receive equal learning opportunities, becoming social justice school leaders. The last section discusses the paucity of literature specifically addressing the preparation of such leaders. A review of the available knowledge reveals that pragmatic approaches to developing transformative leaders, some of which are presented in this book, are still needed.

THE INFLUENCE OF SCHOOL PRINCIPALS

School leadership plays a pivotal role in improving student learning, and its greatest influence is sensed in schools with the greatest need. Leithwood, Harris, and Hopkins (2008) noted that "school leadership is second only to classroom teaching as an influence on pupil learning" (p. 27). Bryk and others (Bryk, Sebring, Allensworth, Luppescu, & Easton, 2010) even argued that "school leadership sits in the first position" (p. 197).

In recent years, the link between school leadership and improved student learning has been empirically proven. The consideration of principalship as a powerful force motivating school effectiveness has been justified by solid evidence. Effective school leaders have been shown to significantly improve student performance, while ineffective principals have a similarly large negative effect (Branch, Hanushek, & Rivkin, 2012; Clark, Martorell, & Rockoff, 2009; Coelli & Green, 2012; Dhuey & Smith, 2014; Grissom & Loeb, 2009; Hallinger & Ko, 2015; Jacobson & Bezzina, 2008). Conducting one of the largest in-depth studies of educational leadership, Louis and her colleagues (2010) argued that school leaders' importance cannot be overemphasized:

> In developing a starting point for this six-year study, we claimed, based on a preliminary review of research, that leadership is second only to classroom instruction as an influence on student learning. After six additional years of research, we are even more confident about this claim. To date we have not found a single case of a school improving its student achievement record in the absence of talented leadership. (p. 9)

To explain why school leadership is of crucial importance, Louis and her colleagues (2010) asserted that most school variables, considered separately, have at most small effects on student outcomes. The real payoff comes when individual variables combine to comprise a critical mass. Creating the conditions under which that can occur is the job of the principal, who generates synergy across the relevant variables, thus creating the potential to unleash the organization's latent capacities.

The principal also fosters a synergy across the various stakeholders of the school, such as teachers, parents, and district personnel, who all strive for students' success by integrating their efforts and activating their respective strengths. Put differently, "the school principal . . . orchestrates the collaborative process of school transformation" (Bryk et al., 2010, p. 203).

Recent research examines not only *whether* school leaders influence student learning but also *how* they generate the improvement of teaching and learning. Findings show that principals impact student performance mainly indirectly (Murphy, Neumerski, Goldring, Grissom, & Porter, 2016), by influencing teachers' strategies (Heck & Hallinger, 2014; Supovitz, Sirinides, & May, 2010) and shaping the environments in which they work (Louis, 2008; May & Supovitz, 2011; Murphy & Torre, 2014).

Looking for specific leadership practices that improve teaching and learning, researchers identified mainly principals' efforts to provide quality professional development, ensure various school programs' coherence, and develop a positive learning climate as associated with differences in classroom instruction and student outcomes (Giles, Jacobson, Johnson, & Ylimaki, 2007; Gimbert & Fultz, 2009; Jacobson, 2011; Sebastian & Allensworth, 2012).

Beyond specific practices, several school leadership approaches were suggested as having the most significant influence on student learning.

The instructional leadership approach emphasizes the principal's deep and direct involvement in teaching and learning (Hallinger & Wang, 2015; May, Huff, & Goldring, 2012). Principals who act as instructional leaders are intensely involved in curricular and instructional issues that in turn directly affect student achievement (Glanz, 2006; Neumerski, 2012).

According to the instructional leadership approach, which may be defined as "the effort to improve teaching and learning for PK–12 students by managing effectively, addressing the challenges of diversity, guiding teacher learning, and fostering organizational learning" (Brazer & Bauer, 2013, p. 650), high-quality instruction, which is a prerequisite for students achieving improved results, requires constant nurturing and guidance by the school's instructional leader (Blase & Kirby, 2009; Stein & Coburn, 2008).

Research has established the existence of links between the principal's instructional leadership and students' achievements (Glickman, Gordon, & Ross-Gordon, 2014). Notably, the effect of instructional leadership on student outcomes was found to be three to four times as great as that of transformational leadership, where leaders inspire, empower, and stimulate teachers (Robinson, Lloyd, & Rowe, 2008).

Another school leadership approach that has been suggested as one that can considerably improve student learning is distributed leadership, that is, increasing the number of people involved in making decisions related to the school's organization, operation, and academic aspects (Lumby, 2013; Robinson, 2008). Such leadership enhances opportunities for the organization to benefit from more of its members' capabilities (Heck & Hallinger, 2009; Malloy & Leithwood, 2017).

Through increased participation in decision-making, a greater commitment to goals and strategies, which leads to student achievement, may develop (Leithwood, Mascall, & Strauss, 2009). The adaption of a distributed approach, under the right conditions, can contribute to organizational development (Harris & DeFlaminis, 2016; Spillane & Coldren, 2011).

School principals can utilize their great influence on teaching and learning to ensure that all students are given equal learning opportunities, irrespective of race, class, gender, ability or disability, sexual orientation, and any other potentially marginalizing conditions. As aforementioned, by organizing their schools to advance all students' equitable learning, principals become social justice leaders.

SOCIAL JUSTICE SCHOOL LEADERS

Recent years have produced an array of literature on social justice in school leadership (Oplatka, 2014). From the perspective of this type of leadership, social justice concepts should be realized in schools so that they provide equal opportunities for all students and treat all students equally, without discrimination or favoritism of any kind (Capper & Frattura, 2007; Wang, 2015).

At the same time, a school is also a means of promoting social justice in the world, since by providing equal opportunities and warranting that no talent is wasted, the school can contribute to the future assignment of individuals to the academic and social positions that correspond to their aptitudes and motivation, regardless of their family's wealth, background, or social belonging (Beachum & McCray, 2010; Bogotch & Shields, 2014). Schools also have a key role in raising active supporters of social justice by enabling students to recognize and question social injustice and encouraging them to be social justice agents who engage in activities that actively seek the promotion of this core value (Jong & Jackson, 2016; Meister, Zimmer, & Wright, 2017).

As for inequalities existing in schools, in most contemporary schools in the Western world, non-white, gay, lesbian, poor, and differently abled students tend to achieve at lower levels and drop out in greater numbers and are also less likely to attend higher education than their white, straight, middle-class, and physically able counterparts (Darling-Hammond, 2010; Ryan, 2016; Sweet, Anisef, Brown, Walters, & Phythian, 2010). Recent accountability-based reforms have hurt mainly the marginalized, particularly the poor and non-white students. These students often find themselves in schools with limited resources, learning via inappropriate methods with teachers who would prefer to be elsewhere (Fabricant & Fine, 2013; Hursh, 2007).

The premise of social justice school leadership is that all students can succeed academically, without exceptions or excuses. By virtue of this belief, social justice leaders transform school environments into spaces where all students thrive, even when it appears that conditions are hopeless, in addition to simultaneously investigating and discovering solutions for issues that generate and reproduce societal inequities (Marshall & Oliva, 2009; Theoharis, 2007, 2008a, 2008b, 2009). Principals with this orientation support students from diverse groups with a wide range of needs (Brooks, Normore, & Wilkinson, 2017; DeMatthews & Mawhinney, 2014), striving for both equity and excellence (Dantley & Tillman, 2010; Jean-Marie, 2008).

Practically, social justice leaders explore differences in academic success between students grouped by race, ethnicity, culture, neighborhood, income of parents, or home language (Johnson & Avelar La Salle, 2010) and work as change agents to eliminate inequities in school policies, procedures, and practices (Brown 2006; McKenzie et al., 2008; Theoharis & Causton-Theoharis, 2008). They emphasize the assignment of students to classrooms so that the proportion of students from every demographic group in each classroom matches that of their proportion in the school (Johnson & Avelar La Salle, 2010).

These leaders also promote teacher practices that are inclusive of varied types of students and their families' perspectives and experiences (Kose, 2007, 2009; Shields, 2004); advocate inclusive education (Lewis, 2016), where services are brought to students in their usual classroom environment rather than in a special resource room, which would involve pulling them out of class to go there (Frattura & Capper, 2009); and "counter the sorting mechanism of schools" (Villegas, 2007, p. 378).

Social justice school leaders claim that exclusionary discipline practices, such as suspension and expulsion, actively remove students from their school communities and exacerbate feelings of isolation and resentment (Losen, 2015). They seek to meet the need for a safe environment while also addressing institutional inequities (Hollie, 2013; Vincent, Randall, Cartledge, Tobin, & Swain-Bradway, 2011), advocating restorative justice in schools (Fronius, Persson, Guckenburg, Hurley, & Petrosino, 2016; Halverson & Kelley, 2017), which is "an approach to discipline that engages all parties in a balanced practice that brings together all people impacted by an issue or behavior" (González, 2012, p. 281). Put differently, the primary aim of a restorative process that takes place in a school is to repair the harm that has been caused by the incident through the active involvement of all stakeholders in discussing what happened and deciding on the appropriate reaction (Normore, 2017).

In the managerial context, social justice school leaders may, for example, work for inclusive decision-making and policymaking processes, help staff members to critically reflect on their practices, and ensure that representatives of various community groups are meaningfully included in school processes (Anderson, 2009; Furman, 2012; Hoffman, 2009). They treat diverse families and communities fairly and equitably by being responsive to their needs as well and not only to the needs of the dominant group (Villegas, 2007). They challenge, deconstruct, and change teachers' negative beliefs and misperceptions about diverse students, families, and communities and thus transform beliefs and values (Theoharis, 2007).

According to Ryan (2016), these sorts of activities constitute "implicit activism," a term referring to social justice activism that attracts little attention. Engaging in explicit activism, which attracts more attention, may be a difficult endeavor for school leaders. Due to their role, they may feel unable to champion social justice, which at times may contradict valued initiatives, violating the culture of their organizations or offending powerful teachers. Their support of social justice initiatives may relegate them to marginal positions within their organization.

While it is widely agreed that social justice school leaders do make a difference, what is less clear is how to prepare principals so that they become such leaders. Quality social justice school leaders require quality preparation;

however, the available knowledge about what such preparation should consist of is insufficient.

PREPARING SOCIAL JUSTICE SCHOOL LEADERS

Existing principal preparation programs are a source of concern to policymakers, university faculty, and educators (Anderson & Reynolds, 2015; Davis & Darling-Hammond, 2012; Gutmore, 2015). Researchers and field personnel have expressed their doubts as to the sufficiency of traditional approaches to preparing and licensing principals (Duncan, Range, & Scherz, 2011; Oplatka & Waite, 2010; Reed & Kensler, 2010), claiming that principal preparation programs do not produce qualified principals who are capable of running schools successfully (Lynch, 2012; Schechter, 2011; Williams, 2015).

Study after study has shown that the training that principals typically receive is not nearly enough to prepare them for their roles (Hernandez, Roberts, & Menchaca, 2012; Pannell Peltier-Glaze, Haynes, Davis, & Skelton, 2015). A recent report revealed that district leaders are generally dissatisfied with the quality of principal preparation programs, and many university professors believe that their programs warrant improvement (Wallace Foundation, 2016).

According to Drago-Severson (2009, 2012; Drago-Severson, Blum-DeStefano, & Asghar, 2013), existing preparation programs involve informational learning, which focuses on increasing the learner's amount of knowledge and skills: "All too often . . . we teach leadership development in the same way we teach world history: by presenting just the facts, just the contents" (Drago-Severson, 2012, p. 8). She claims that for preparation programs to be most effective, they should involve transformational learning, which "relates to the development of the cognitive, emotional, interpersonal and intrapersonal capacities that enable a person to manage the complexities of work (e.g., leadership, teaching, learning, adaptive challenges) and life" (Drago-Severson, 2009, p. 11). In view of the broad criticism of existing preparation programs, understanding how to better prepare preservice principals for their future role is an urgent policy concern.

When it comes to preparing prospective principals in traditional preparation programs to become social justice leaders, only token consideration is given to social justice concerns (Cambron-McCabe & McCarthy, 2005). In many preparation programs, most diversity-related education occurs in a single course and centers on broad societal conditions that affect students, such as discrimination, inequitable school resources, and poverty, rather than providing aspiring principals with the skills needed to actually address these inequities in schools. Teaching social justice is often left to the discretion of individual faculty members, who are not necessarily experts in this field (Hawley & James, 2010).

In order to properly train social justice school leaders, preparation programs should integrate social justice knowledge, attitudes, and skills throughout curriculum, instruction, and assessment, rather than offering in a single, add-on course (McKenzie et al., 2008; Zembylas, 2010). They must move beyond surface-level knowledge to engage prospective principals at the critical or transformative level (Lopez, 2010) using a variety of instructional methods (Brown, 2004, 2006; Theoharis, 2007).

Faculty should develop a commitment to social justice, which "require[s] faculty to rethink underlying assumptions, actions and policies, roles and relationships, pedagogical approaches, and levels of preparedness that challenge current modes of operation and force faculty to answer why and for whom" (Byrne-Jimenez, 2010, p. 6). Preparation programs should provide professional development in the area of social justice to faculty (Rusch, 2004) and make human resource practices diversity-conscious, hiring more faculty of color (Young & Brooks, 2008).

Practically, Capper, Theoharis, and Sebastian (2006) proposed a framework for preparing school leaders for social justice leadership. The horizontal dimension of their framework describes what principals must believe, know, and do as social justice leaders, including three domains: (1) critical consciousness, (2) knowledge, and (3) practical skills focused on social justice. To achieve these ends, the vertical dimensions of the framework are curriculum, pedagogy, and assessment oriented toward social justice. Guerra, Nelson, Jacobs, and Yamamura (2013) pointed to programmatic elements that assist the development of social justice leaders during principal preparation, including developing awareness of their identity, reading literature that highlights inequities in schools, participating in intense classroom conversations where their thinking is challenged by professors and peers, and leading and implementing action research projects.

The literature on the preparation of social justice school leaders reviewed in this section is significant albeit limited in scope. The existing research provides only general guidelines for social justice leadership training, leaving much to be desired.

CONCLUSION

The research is clear: principals' impact on student learning is great. School leadership is the second most important school-based factor in students' academic achievements (Bryk et al., 2010; Leithwood et al., 2008; Louis et al., 2010). The great influence of a principal furnishes the rationale for social justice school leadership, where principals utilize their influence to ensure that all students are provided equal opportunities for quality learning, regardless of race, gender, religion, national origin, ability or disability, sexual orientation, age, or other potentially marginalizing characteristics (Marshall & Oliva, 2009; Theoharis, 2009).

Social justice school leaders actively assure that all students thrive, even when chances for this seem slim (Brooks, Normore, & Wilkinson, 2017; DeMatthews & Mawhinney, 2014). The question then arises: what is the optimal training necessary for producing social justice school leaders? Unfortunately, recent literature, partially reviewed in this chapter, does not provide satisfactory answers to this question. The existing body of knowledge concerning the preparation of social justice school leaders is insufficient. For this reason, workable approaches to developing leaders who are effective in achieving social justice, equity, and excellence are still necessary, as they can be most useful for those who wish to improve contemporary school systems.

KEY IDEAS IN THIS CHAPTER

1. *Principals' great impact on student learning is clearly proven in the literature. School leadership's effectiveness is crucial to improving student outcomes, and its greatest influence is felt in schools with the greatest need. Several school leadership approaches were suggested as having the most significant influence on student learning, such as instructional leadership and distributed leadership.*
2. *The principal's significant impact constitutes the conceptual basis for social justice school leadership, where school leaders ascertain that all students are provided equal opportunities for quality learning, irrespective of race, gender, religion, national origin, ability or disability, sexual orientation, age, or any other potentially marginalizing characteristics.*
3. *The available knowledge regarding the optimal way to prepare social justice school leaders is still limited. Recent literature does not provide satisfactory answers to the question of how school leaders are to be prepared for their social justice role.*

REFERENCES

Anderson, G. (2009). *Advocacy leadership: Toward a post-reform agenda in education.* New York, NY: Routledge.

Anderson, E., & Reynolds, A. L. (2015). *A policymaker's guide: Research-based policy for principal preparation program approval and licensure.* Charlottesville, VA: University Council of Educational Administration.

Beachum, F., & McCray, C. R. (2010). Cracking the code: Illuminating the promises and pitfalls of social justice in educational leadership. *International Journal of Urban Educational Leadership, 4*(1), 206–221.

Blase, J., & Kirby, P. (2009). *Bringing out the best in teachers: What effective principals do.* Thousand Oaks, CA: Corwin.

Bogotch, I., & Shields, C. M. (2014). Do promises of social justice trump paradigms of educational leadership? In I. Bogotch & C. M. Shields (Eds.), *International handbook of educational leadership and social (in)justice* (pp. 1–12). Dordrecht, The Netherlands: Springer.

Branch, G. F., Hanushek, E. A., & Rivkin, S. G. (2012). *Estimating the effect of leaders on public sector productivity: The case of school principals. NBER Working Paper 17803.* Cambridge, MA: National Bureau of Economic Research.

Brazer, S. D., & Bauer, S. C. (2013). Preparing instructional leaders: A model. *Educational Administration Quarterly, 49*(4), 645–684.

Brooks, J. S., Normore, A. H., & Wilkinson, J. (2017). School leadership, social justice and immigration: Examining, exploring and extending two frameworks. *International Journal of Educational Management, 31*(5), 679–690.

Brown, K. M. (2004). Leadership for social justice and equity: Weaving and pedagogy. *Educational Administration Quarterly, 40*(1), 77–108.

Brown, K. M. (2006). Leadership for social justice and equity: Evaluating a transformative framework and andragogy. *Educational Administration Quarterly, 42*(5), 700–745.

Bryk, A. S., Sebring, P. B., Allensworth, E., Luppescu, S., & Easton, J. Q. (2010). *Organizing schools for improvement: Lessons from Chicago.* Chicago, IL: University of Chicago Press.

Byrne-Jimenez, M. (2010). Point/counterpoint: Preparing leaders for diversity. *UCEA Review, 51*(3), 6.

Cambron-McCabe, N., & McCarthy, M. M. (2005). Educating school leaders for social justice. *Educational Policy, 19*(1), 201–222.

Capper, C. A., Theoharis, G., & Sebastian, J. (2006). Toward a framework for preparing leaders for social justice. *Journal of Educational Administration, 44*(3), 209–224.

Capper, E. M., & Frattura, C. A. (2007). *Leading for social justice: Transforming schools for all learners.* Thousand Oaks, CA: Corwin Press.

Clark, D., Martorell, P., & Rockoff, J. (2009). *School principals and school performance. Working Paper 38.* Washington, DC: Urban Institute.

Coelli, M., & Green, D. (2012). Leadership effects: School principals and student outcomes. *Economics of Education Review, 31*(1), 92–109.

Dantley, M. E., & Tillman, L. C. (2010). Social justice and moral transformative leadership. In C. Marshall & M. Oliva (Eds.), *Leadership for social justice* (2nd ed., pp. 19–34). Boston, MA: Allyn & Bacon.

Darling-Hammond, L. (2010). *The flat world and education: How America's commitment to equity will determine our future.* New York, NY: Teachers College Press.

Davis, S. H., & Darling-Hammond, L. (2012). Innovative principal preparation programs: What works and how we know. *Planning and Changing, 43*(1–2), 25–45.

DeMatthews, D., & Mawhinney, H. (2014). Social justice leadership and inclusion:
Exploring challenges in an urban district struggling to address inequities. *Educational Administration Quarterly, 50*(5), 844–881.

Dhuey, E., & Smith, J. (2014). How important are principals in the production of
school achievement? *Canadian Journal of Economics, 47*(2), 634–663.

Drago-Severson, E. (2009). *Leading adult learning: Supporting adult development in
our schools*. Thousand Oaks, CA: Corwin.

Drago-Severson, E. (2012). *Helping educators grow: Strategies and practices for
leadership development*. Cambridge, MA: Harvard.

Drago-Severson, E., Blum-DeStefano, J., & Asghar, A. (2013). *Learning for leadership: Developmental strategies for building capacity in our schools*. Thousand
Oaks, CA: Corwin.

Duncan, H., Range, B., & Scherz, S. (2011). From professional preparation to on-
the-job development: What do beginning principals need? *International Journal of
Educational Leadership Preparation, 6*(3).

Fabricant, M., & Fine, M. (2013). *The changing politics of education: Privatization
and the dispossessed lives left behind*. Boulder, CO: Paradigm.

Frattura, C. A., & Capper, E. M. (2009). *Meeting the needs of students of all abilities:
How leaders go beyond inclusion* (2nd ed.). Thousand Oaks, CA: Corwin.

Fronius, T., Persson, H., Guckenburg, S., Hurley, N., & Petrosino, A. (2016). *Restorative justice in US schools: A research review*. San Francisco, CA: WestEd.

Furman, G. (2012). Social justice leadership as praxis: Developing capacities through
preparation programs. *Educational Administration Quarterly, 48*(2), 191–229.

Giles, C., Jacobson, S., Johnson, L., & Ylimaki, R. (2007). Against the odds: successful principals in challenging US schools. In C. Day & K. Leithwood (Eds.),
Successful principal leadership in times of change: An international perspective
(pp. 155–168). Dordrecht, The Netherlands: Springer.

Gimbert, B., & Fultz, D. (2009). Effective principal leadership for beginning teacher
development. *International Journal of Educational Leadership Preparation, 4*(2),
1–15.

Glanz, J. (2006). *Instructional Leadership*. Thousand Oaks, CA: Corwin.

Glickman, C. D., Gordon, S. P., & Ross-Gordon, J. M. (2014). *Supervision and
instructional leadership: A developmental approach* (9th ed.). London, UK:
Pearson.

González, T. (2012). Keeping kids in schools: Restorative justice, punitive discipline,
and the school to prison pipeline. *Journal of Law & Education, 41*(2), 281–335.

Grissom, J. A., & Loeb, S. (2009). *Triangulating principal effectiveness: How perspectives of parents, teachers, and assistant principals identify the central importance of managerial skills. Working Paper 35*. Washington, DC: Urban Institute.

Guerra, P. L., Nelson, S. W., Jacobs, J., & Yamamura, E. (2013). Developing educational leaders for social justice: Programmatic elements that work or need improvement. *Education Research and Perspectives, 40*(1), 124–149.

Gutmore, D. (2015). Principal preparation—revisited—time matters. *AASA Journal
of Scholarship & Practice, 12*(3), 4–10.

Hallinger, P., & Ko, J. (2015). Education accountability and principal leadership effects in Hong Kong primary schools. *Nordic Journal of Studies in Educational Policy, 3*, 18–29.

Hallinger, P., & Wang, W. C. (2015). *Assessing instructional leadership with the Principal Instructional Management Rating Scale.* Dordrecht, The Netherlands: Springer.

Halverson, R., & Kelley, C. (2017). *Mapping leadership: The tasks that matter for improving teaching and learning in schools.* San Francisco, CA: Jossey Bass.

Harris, A., & DeFlaminis, J. (2016). Distributed leadership in practice: Evidence, misconceptions and possibilities. *Management in Education, 30*(4), 141–146.

Hawley, W., & James, R. (2010). Diversity-responsive school leadership. *UCEA Review, 51*(3), 1–5.

Heck, R. H., & Hallinger, P. (2009). Assessing the contribution of distributed leadership to school improvement and growth in math achievement. *American educational Research Journal, 46*(3), 659–689.

Heck, R. H., & Hallinger, P. (2014). Modeling the longitudinal effects of school leadership on teaching and learning over time. *Journal of Educational Administration, 52*(5), 653–681.

Hernandez, R., Roberts, M., & Menchaca, V. (2012). Redesigning a principal preparation program: A continuous improvement model. *International Journal of Educational Leadership, 7*(3).

Hoffman, L. (2009). Educational leadership and social activism: A call for action. *Journal of Educational Administration and History, 41*(4), 391–410.

Hollie, S. (2013). *Culturally and linguistically responsive teaching and learning: Classroom practices for student success.* Huntington Beach, CA: Shell.

Hursh, D. (2007). Assessing no child left behind and the rise of neoliberal education policies. *American Educational Research Journal, 44*(3), 493–518.

Jacobson, S. (2011). Leadership effects on student achievement and sustained school success. *International Journal of Educational Management, 25*(1), 33–44.

Jacobson, S., & Bezzina, C. (2008). The effects of leadership on student academic/affective achievement. In G. Crow, J. Lumby, & P. Pashiardis (Eds.), *The international handbook on the preparation and development of school leaders* (pp. 80–102). Thousand Oaks, CA: Sage.

Jean-Marie, G. (2008). Leadership for social justice: An agenda for 21st century schools. *The Educational Forum, 72*(4), pp. 340–354.

Johnson, R. S., & Avelar La Salle, R. (2010). *Data strategies to uncover and eliminate hidden inequities: The wallpaper effect.* Thousand Oaks, CA: Corwin.

Jong, C., & Jackson, C. (2016). Teaching mathematics for social justice: Examining preservice teachers' conceptions. *Journal of Mathematics Education at Teachers College, 7*(1), 27–34.

Kose, B. W. (2007). Principal leadership for social justice: Uncovering the content of teacher professional development. *Journal of School Leadership, 17*(3), pp. 276–312.

Kose, B. W. (2009). The principal's role in professional development for social justice: An empirically-based transformative framework. *Urban Education, 44*(6), 628–663.

Leithwood, K., Harris, A., & Hopkins, D. (2008). Seven strong claims about successful school leadership. *School Leadership & Management, 28*(1), 27–42.

Leithwood, K., Mascall, B., & Strauss, T. (Eds.) (2009). *Distributed leadership according to the evidence*. New York, NY: Routledge.

Lewis, K. (2016). Social justice leadership and inclusion: A genealogy. *Journal of Educational Administration and History, 48*(4), 324–341.

Lopez, G. (2010). Mainstreaming diversity? "What'chu talking about, Willis?" *UCEA Review, 51*(3), 6–8.

Losen, D. J. (2015). *Closing the school discipline gap: Equitable remedies for excessive exclusion*. New York, NY: Teachers College.

Louis, K. S. (2008). Learning to support improvement—next steps for research on district practice. *American Journal of Education, 114*(4), 681–689.

Louis, K. S., Leithwood, K., Wahlstrom, K. L., & Anderson, L. E. (2010). *Learning from leadership: Investigating the links to improved student learning*. New York, NY: Wallace Foundation.

Lumby, J. (2013). Distributed leadership: The uses and abuses of power. *Educational Management Administration & Leadership, 41*(5), 581–597.

Lynch, J. M. (2012). Responsibilities of today's principal: Implications for principal preparation programs and principal certification policies. *Rural Special Education Quarterly, 31*(2), 40–47.

Malloy, J., & Leithwood, K. (2017). Effects of distributed leadership on school academic press and student achievement. In: K. Leithwood, J. Sun, & K. Pollock (Eds.), *How school leaders contribute to student success: Studies in educational leadership, vol. 23* (pp. 69–91). Cham, Switzerland: Springer.

Marshall, C., & Oliva, M. (Eds.) (2009). *Leadership for social justice: Making revolutions in education* (2nd ed.). Boston, MA: Pearson.

May, H., Huff, J., & Goldring, E. (2012). A longitudinal study of principals' activities and student performance. *School Effectiveness and School Improvement, 23*(4), 417–439.

May, H., & Supovitz, J. A. (2011). The scope of principal efforts to improve instruction. *Educational Administration Quarterly, 47*(2), 332–352.

McKenzie, K. B., Christman, D. E., Hernandez, F., Fierro, E., Capper, C. A., Dantley, M., ... Scheurich, J. J. (2008). From the field: A proposal for educating leaders for social justice. *Educational Administration Quarterly, 44*(1), 111–138.

Meister, S. M., Zimmer, W. K., & Wright, K. L. (2017). Social justice in practitioner publications: A systematic literature review. *Journal of Urban Learning, Teaching, and Research, 13*, 90–111.

Murphy, J., Neumerski, C. M., Goldring, E., Grissom, J., & Porter, A. (2016). Bottling fog? The quest for instructional management. *Cambridge Journal of Education, 46*(4), 455–471.

Murphy, J., & Torre, D. (2014). *Creating productive cultures in schools: For students, teachers, and parents*. Thousand Oaks, CA: Corwin.

Neumerski, C. M. (2012). Rethinking instructional leadership, a review: What do we know about principal, teacher, and coach instructional leadership, and where should we go from here? *Educational Administration Quarterly, 49*(2), 310–347.

Normore, A. H. (2017). Social justice and restorative processes in urban schools: Historical context. In A. H. Normore (Ed.), *Restorative practice meets social justice* (pp. 1–18). Charlotte, NC: Information Age.

Oplatka, I. (2014). The place of "social justice" in the field of educational administration: A journal-based historical overview of emergent area of study. In I. Bogotch & C. M. Shields (Eds.), *International handbook of educational leadership and social (in)justice* (pp. 15–35). Dordrecht, The Netherlands: Springer.

Oplatka, I., & Waite, D. (2010). The new principal preparation program model in Israel: Ponderings about practice-oriented principal training. In A. H. Normore (Ed.), *Global perspectives on educational leadership reform: The development and preparation of leaders of learning and learners of leadership—Advances in Educational Administration, Volume 11* (pp. 47–66). Bingley, UK: Emerald Group Publishing.

Pannell, S., Peltier-Glaze, B. M., Haynes, I., Davis, D., & Skelton, C. (2015). Evaluating the effectiveness of traditional and alternative principal preparation programs. *Journal of Organizational and Educational Leadership, 1*(2).

Reed, C. J., & Kensler, L. A. W. (2010). Creating a new system for principal preparation: Reflections on efforts to transcend tradition and create new cultures. *Journal of Research on Leadership Education, 5*(12.10), 568–582.

Robinson, V. M. J. (2008). Forging the links between distributed leadership and educational outcomes. *Journal of Educational Administration, 46*(2), 241–256.

Robinson, V. M. J., Lloyd, C., & Rowe, K. (2008). The impact of leadership on student outcomes: An analysis of the differential effects of leadership types. *Educational Administration Quarterly, 44*(5), 564–588.

Rusch, E. A. (2004). Gender and race in leadership preparation: A constrained discourse. *Educational Administration Quarterly, 40*(1), 16–48.

Ryan, J. (2016). Strategic activism, educational leadership and social justice. *International Journal of Leadership in Education, 19*(1), 87–100.

Schechter, C. (2011). Switching cognitive gears: Problem-based learning and success-based learning as instructional frameworks in leadership education. *Journal of Educational Administration, 49*(2), 143–165.

Sebastian, J., & Allensworth, E. (2012). The influence of principal leadership on classroom instruction and student learning: A study of mediated pathways to learning. *Educational Administration Quarterly, 48*(4), 626–663.

Shields, C. M. (2004). Dialogic leadership for social justice: Overcoming pathologies of silence. *Educational Administration Quarterly, 40*(1), 109–132.

Spillane, J., & Coldren, A. F. (2011). *Diagnosis and design for school improvement.* New York, NY: Teachers College.

Stein, M. K., & Coburn, C. E. (2008). Architectures for learning: A comparative analysis of two urban school districts. *American Journal of Education, 114*(8), 583–626.

Supovitz, J., Sirinides, P., & May, H. (2010). How principals and peers influence teaching and learning. *Educational Administration Quarterly, 46*(1), 31–56.

Sweet, R., Anisef, P., Brown, R., Walters, D., & Phythian, K. (2010). *Post-high school pathways of immigrant youth.* Toronto: Higher Education Quality Council of Ontario.

Theoharis, G. (2007). Social justice educational leaders and resistance: Toward a theory of social justice leadership. *Educational Administration Quarterly*, *43*(2), 221–258.

Theoharis, G. (2008a). Woven in deeply: Identity and leadership of urban social justice principals. *Education and Urban Society*, *41*(1), 3–25.

Theoharis, G. (2008b). "At every turn": The resistance that principals face in their pursuit of equity and justice. *Journal of School Leadership*, *18*(3), pp. 303–343.

Theoharis, G. (2009). *The school leaders our children deserve: Seven keys to equity, social justice, and school reform*. New York, NY: Teachers College.

Theoharis, G., & Causton-Theoharis, J. N. (2008). Oppressors or emancipators: Critical dispositions for preparing inclusive school leaders. *Equity and Excellence in Education*, *41*(2), 230–246.

Villegas, A. M. (2007). Disposition in teacher education: A look at social justice. *Journal of Teacher Education*, *50*(5), 370–380.

Vincent, C., Randall, C., Cartledge, G., Tobin, T., & Swain-Bradway, J. (2011). Toward a conceptual integration of cultural responsiveness and schoolwide positive behavior support. *Journal of Positive Behavior Interventions*, *13*(4), 219–229.

Wallace Foundation (2016). *Improving university principal preparation programs: Five themes from the field*. New York, NY: Wallace Foundation.

Wang, F. (2015). Conceptualizing social justice: Interviews with principals. *Journal of Educational Administration*, *53*(5), 667–681.

Williams, S. M. (2015). The future of principal preparation and principal evaluation: Reflections of the current policy context for school leaders. *Journal of Research on Leadership Education*, *10*(3), 222–225.

Young, M. D., & Brooks, J. S. (2008). Supporting graduate students of colour in educational administration preparation programs: Faculty perspectives on best practices, possibilities, and problems. *Educational Administration Quarterly*, *44*(3), 391–423.

Zembylas, M. (2010). The emotional aspects of leadership for social justice: Implications for leadership preparation programs. *Journal of Educational Administration*, *48*(5), 611–625.

Section II

TRANSFORMATIVE ANDRAGOGICAL PRACTICE AND THE CENTRALITY OF EXPERIENCE

Chapter 4

Awareness of Self through Critical Reflection

INTRODUCTION

"Once a mind is expanded by a better idea it can never return to its original form"

—(Oliver Wendell Holmes).

Developing as a critically reflective administrator encompasses both the capacity for *critical inquiry* and *self-reflection* (Larrivee, 2000; Schon, 1987). Critical inquiry involves the conscious consideration of the moral and ethical implications and consequences of schooling practices on students. Self-reflection adds the dimension of deep examination of personal assumptions, values, and beliefs. *Critical reflection* merges the two terms and involves the examination of personal and professional belief systems, as well as the deliberate consideration of the ethical implications and impact of practices. According to Mezirow (1991), "reflection is the process of critically assessing the content, process or premise(s) of our efforts to interpret and give meaning to an experience" (p. 104).

In this chapter, four andragogical strategies for raising consciousness (Educational Leadership Constituent Council (ELCC) dimension of Awareness); stimulating transformative learning; and developing future leaders for social justice, equity, and excellence are presented. Adult learners who (1) write in reflective analysis journals, (2) complete cultural autobiographies, (3) participate in prejudice reduction workshops, and (4) organize and facilitate diversity presentations and panels engage in self-directed, experiential learning. By learning how to learn, they improve their ability to identify ontological and epistemological assumptions, to understand multiple perspectives, and to expand their "worldview."

REFLECTIVE ANALYSIS JOURNALS

Reflection is at the heart of transformative learning. The development of critical thinking and open-mindedness requires a critical stance toward established paradigms and an openness to alternative viewpoints. Dewey (1910) noted that "the essence of critical thinking is suspended judgment; and the essence of this suspense is inquiry" (p. 74).

According to Brookfield (1995), "critical reflection is not just a process of hunting assumptions of power and hegemony by viewing what we do through different lenses" (p. 207). It is also an idea with an impressive intellectual pedigree, including elements of critical theory, psychoanalysis, phenomenology, and pragmatism. Journal writing has been incorporated throughout these disciplines as a means of self-expression.

In preparation programs, self-reflection and transformative learning are enhanced through the use of a dialogue journal and the use of self-analysis (Cranton, 1994). In a dialogue journal, either the professor or adult cohort members respond to the journal entries with comments and critical questions. Learner self-analysis of the journal stimulates further self-reflection and self-directed learning. Future leaders are then instructed to examine the journal for patterns and themes in content and for changes in opinions, thinking, or feelings over time (i.e., during the course of a semester).

Journaling makes the invisible thoughts visible. Adult learners are encouraged to complete reflective analysis journals throughout the course of their graduate program as a means of identifying and clarifying thoughts, feelings, beliefs, perspectives, worldviews, challenges, hopes, and aspirations. Through journaling, future leaders expand their awareness, make connections, and generate new thoughts. They identify principles and approaches learned, explain how this new information might be applied, and explore these discoveries in light of personal and professional growth and development.

Adult learners are encouraged to share their entries via class and online chat rooms. The dialogue is rational and ongoing, challenging but not judgmental, provocative but not condescending. Through journal writing, self-reflection, and critical inquiry future leaders for social justice, equity, and excellence reportedly began to question and modify previously taken-for-granted frames of reference.

Self-Reflection

The current study indicated that as some future leaders examined and reevaluated their experiences and expectations, they came to a deeper understanding of themselves. Accordingly, they perceived and valued the alternative andragogical strategies employed as growth-inducing, perspective-shifting, and life-changing.

> I see myself as one who is enlightened, yet the biggest surprise is my heightened awareness of my prejudices, my perceptions, and my "close-minded" liberalism that shapes the way I live my life. I realized how biased I really am deep down inside. I realized that many of my beliefs are racist and many of my thoughts are close-minded. Although this self-realization is a hard pill to swallow, there is nothing but positive that can come from this discovery.
>
> While it is easier to see the practicality of our graduate classes in supervision, leadership, and curriculum alignment, my societal perceptions, my understanding of education's root problems, and the way in which I interact with others has really changed.
>
> I delight in stretching myself and discovering things, misconceptions, ideas, thoughts, assumptions that need to be dealt with.
>
> I think that I am not the same leader I was before I entered the MSA program, or the same person for that matter. I have been exposed to new ideas that guide my thinking. . . . I've learned the importance of reflective practice.
>
> The panel really had an impact on me today. Like Janeka, I too struggle between the Malcolm X and MLK Jr. response. I realized that her poise in handling the racist teacher accomplished a lot more than my knee-jerk anger would have. I must remember this often, especially as an administrator.

The process of transforming meaning structures is a complex, arduous task. While several future leaders reported being "exhausted on many fronts, physically and emotionally," they were also grateful for the experience because it made them " 'push through' both academically and personally." Recognizing that race is a difficult topic to discuss, that their comfort zones were being tested, and that they were learning a "cathartic lesson," a few adult learners became more acutely aware of their deeply engrained fears. One young male wrote, "I am afraid that if I shared how I felt on certain issues that I might be mistakenly referred to as inflexible and possibly, even indirectly racist." Other students articulated similar sentiments:

> I am really nervous now. Some of my views concerning some aspects of education are not the same as what I think I am going to be taught. I am getting a little confused.
>
> Today's class was definitely the most difficult for me to be open in my participation to date. Discussions along the lines of race have always been difficult for me to partake in due to my fear of saying something that might be interpreted the wrong way by a member of the minority group and it resulting in me being labeled thereafter. Class discussions definitely get heated at times. And yet, in relation to my preparation as an administrator, my ability to lead discussions on topics of race and the obstacles that minorities have been forced to overcome

in past and current U.S. educational history is vital to my success as a school leader.

Unfortunately, as I was learning to listen openly to others and to love the diversity around me, I shuddered at the thought of allowing people to get to know me. What if I said the wrong things? What if they judged me by my skin color or dialect? What if many of these good people born in the Bible belt lost respect in me because I said that I was questioning my faith? Will they accept who I was yesterday, who I am today, and who I will be tomorrow?

Critical Inquiry

As future leaders' awareness of themselves and their inner thoughts and feelings began to change, they began to question the treatment of others. According to one student, "I have been awakened to the whole idea of schools being used to socialize, train, and pigeon-hole people. I am 45 years old and still so naïve." Through reflection, many of the adult learners became more critically conscious of oppressive practices and their responsibility to change them.

Is it possible that I have been participating in a system that sorts, chooses, and places members of ethnic and socioeconomic groups into pre-destined positions in our society? I learned that the answer could be "absolutely" and that it will be my job to be more aware of these trends as I enter my role as an administrator.

I look at myself in the scheme of things and realize that I am very guilty of upholding some of the very biases that I read about by indirectly not saying or doing more.

It has taken almost half the semester for me to "get it." I finally understand why we are learning about the history of minority groups and their educational experience. I thought and believed that because I am a member of a minority group and I empathize with their struggles, that I was already committed to equitable education for all.

Maybe my first thoughts of what I could learn about "our" plight were wrong or misguided because now I feel a growing responsibility to learn about others' plights and how I can end some of the "drama" for them.

I was at first enthralled by the info, next came anger, and lastly sadness as I realized that this agenda is still in effect and I am on some level aware of it and have used it to my advantage. Am I just as guilty for/of somehow upholding the biased standard of "maintaining the status quo?" Will I be able to change the system?

CULTURAL AUTOBIOGRAPHIES

Self-awareness regarding one's culture and background has been identified as a key prerequisite and a first step for learners in multicultural programs (Brown, Parham, & Yonker, 1996; York, 1994). Banks (1994) and others suggested that individuals do not become sensitive and open to different ethnic groups until and unless they develop a positive sense of self, including an awareness and acceptance of their own ethnic group.

When adults learn about their heritage and contributions to society, they participate in a process of self-discovery and growth in social consciousness, what Freire (1970) called "critical consciousness" (see "Critical Social Theory" section in chapter 2). Indeed, as Miller (1998) suggested, "by encouraging an educator to examine disjunctures, ruptures, break-ups, and fractures in . . . her own and others' educational practices, autobiography can function to 'queer' or to make theory, practice, *and* the self *unfamiliar*" (p. 370).

By completing cultural autobiographies, future leaders begin to identify and name particular vantage points through which all their experiences and perceptions have been filtered. What perhaps had previously been an "unexamined backdrop for everyday life" (Delpit, 1995, p. 92) becomes more explicit as adult learners research their home culture, their language, their socioeconomic status, their formal and informal education (including the hidden curriculum), and their demographic characteristics (i.e., age, gender, race, ethnicity, sexual orientation, class, abilities) relative to the dominant culture.

Because Coleman and Deutsch (1995) found that "issues unique to interethnic conflict emerge from cultural misunderstandings, ethnocentrism, long-held stereotypes, and the importance of ethnic identity to self identity" (p. 387), future leaders for social justice, equity, and excellence are encouraged to examine their own self-identities and remember that:

> The best solutions will arise from the acceptance that alternative worldviews exist—that there are valid alternative means to any end, as well as valid alternative ends in themselves. We all interpret behaviors, information, and situations through our own cultural lenses; these lenses operate involuntarily, below the level of conscious awareness, making it seem that our own view is simply "the way it is." Learning to interpret across cultures demands reflecting on our own experiences, analyzing our own culture, examining and comparing varying perspectives. We must consciously and voluntarily make our cultural lenses apparent. (Delpit, 1995, p. 151)

Racial and Cultural Identity Development

The construct of *racial and cultural identity* describes our inclination to identify (or not identify) with the racial/cultural group to which we are assumed to belong. Our racial/cultural identity is a reflection of how we see ourselves, those with whom we share racial classification, and those whom we perceive to be outside our racial/cultural group (Carter, 1997; Cross, 1994).

Racial identity development also helps to dispel the cultural conformity myth that all individuals from a particular minority group are the same with the same attitudes and preferences. In essence, racial/cultural identity development asserts differences in individual development. It is shaped and influenced by a variety of internal and external environmental factors, including social messages about the individual's worth as well as that of his or her group, parental socialization concerning race relations, peer influences, and educators' communications about race and racial differences.

For most individuals, racial/cultural identity does not emerge until adolescence because a level of cognitive maturity is required to comprehend the relative permanence of racial classification and racial group membership (Phinney, 1993). Regardless of when or how it begins, it has become increasingly evident that identity development or establishing a stable sense of self-concept is an essential developmental task.

Researchers found that an achieved identity is associated with positive psychological outcomes, including self-assurance, self-certainty, and a sense of mastery (Adams, Gullotta, & Montemayor, 1992; Marcia, Waterman, Matteson, Archer, & Orlofsky, 1994; Phinney, Cantu, & Curtz, 1997). Because there is also evidence to suggest a positive relationship between identity formation and academic success (Berzonsky & Kuk, 2000), it is important for future leaders to understand identity development for themselves, as well as for their teachers, students, and parents.

In perhaps the most cited work on adolescent race and identity development, Erikson (1968) pointed out the likelihood that members of an "oppressed and exploited minority" (p. 303) may internalize the negative views of the dominant society, thereby developing a negative identity and self-hatred. Social psychologists expressed similar concerns by suggesting that membership in a disparaged minority group can create psychological conflict (Tajfel, 1978).

As a result, minority group members are faced with a choice of accepting the negative views of society toward their group or rejecting them in search of their own identity. Understanding the meaning and implications of these differences and making decisions about how to live with their dual cultural heritage, values, and status are part of racial/cultural identity formation. So too is the ability to negotiate and establish feelings of self-worth in the face of conflicting messages, discrimination, and stereotyping.

Most identity development models and theories trace their roots to either the psychosocial research of Erikson (1959/1980), the identity formation studies of Marcia (1980), or the cognitive structural work of Piaget (1952). Traditional identity models are stage models in which growth occurs linearly in stepwise progression, whereas contemporary models describe racial and cultural identity as a process that occurs over a lifetime.

Specifically speaking, racial identity theory concerns a person's self-conception of herself or himself as a racial being, as well as one's beliefs, attitudes, and values vis-à-vis oneself relative to racial groups other than one's own. Most of the theory and research has focused on African Americans and their understanding of the black experience in the United States. Cross's (1978, 1995) model of *nigrescence* is considered one of the first and most prevalent models of racial identity development theory.

The term *nigrescence* can be defined as a "resocialization experience" (Cross, 1995, p. 97), in which a healthy black person progresses from a non-Afrocentric to an Afrocentric to a multicultural identity. During this transformation, Cross posited that a person ideally moves from a complete unawareness of race through embracing black culture exclusively toward a commitment to many cultures and a desire to address the concerns of all oppressed groups. He characterized these five stages as (1) pre-encounter, (2) encounter, (3) immersion/emersion, (4) internalization, and (5) internalization/commitment (Cross, 1978).

Parham (1989) also studied African Americans and described cycles of racial identity development as a lifelong, continuously changing process. His theory is that blacks move through angry feelings about whites and develop positive frames of reference. Ideally this progression from an unconscious to a conscious racial identity leads to a realistic perception of one's self and to bicultural success. Although these theories and those of others who have studied African Americans (e.g., Jackson, 1975; Parham & Helms, 1981) can be problematic for different reasons, the transference to a healthy, racial self is critically important. The concept of racial identity is a surface-level manifestation often based on what we look like (e.g., skin color), yet it has deep implications for how we are treated (O'Hearn, 1998).

According to Chavez and Guido-DiBrito (1999) identity formation is often triggered by two conflicting social and cultural influences. "First, deep conscious immersion into cultural traditions and values through religious, familial, neighborhood, and educational communities instills a positive sense of ethnic identity and confidence. Second, and in contrast, individuals often filter ethnic identity through negative treatment and media messages received from others because of their race and ethnicity" (p. 39). For people with minority status, such messages are clear—you are different, and your ethnic makeup is less than desirable within mainstream society.

Helms (1993, 1994, 1995) developed one of the first white racial identity models. Her model presupposes the existence of white superiority and individual, cultural, and institutional racism. Instead of limited stages, Helms referred to the status of white racial identity. Her first three statuses outline how a white individual progresses away from a racist frame before moving to the next three statuses where he or she discovers a nonracist white identity. Helms outlines interracial exposure as a powerful trigger. Problematic is her notion that racial identity for whites is about their perceptions, feelings, and behaviors toward blacks versus the development and consciousness of an actual white racial identity. While Katz (1989) and Ponterotto and Pedersen (1993) also researched Caucasians, Helms (1993) differentiated between theories of black racial identity and white racial identity in the following manner:

> Black racial identity theories . . . explain the various ways . . . Blacks can identify (or not identify) with other Blacks and/or adopt or abandon identities resulting from racial victimization; white racial identity theories . . . explain the various ways . . . whites can identify (or not identify) with other whites and/or evolve or avoid evolving a nonoppressive white identity. (p. 5)

Regardless of color, all racial identity models discuss an intersection between racial perceptions of others (racism) and racial perception of self (racial identity). Since the earlier studies on African Americans, researchers have developed numerous models of racial identity development among other groups (Cross, 1994). For example, Lee (1988) and Kim (1981) explored Asian American identity development, Arce (1981) tried to better understand Chicano identity, and Garrett and Walking Stick Garrett (1994) and Horse (2001) researched Native American identity development, while Gibbs (1987) examined identity differences of biracial students, and Cass (1979) applied similar theories to homosexual identity development. See table 4.1 for a sample of these and other racial and cultural identity development models.

Phinney's Three-Stage Model of Ethnic Identity Development

Similar to ego and racial identity theories, ethnic identity development models focus on what and how oppressed people come to understand themselves in terms of their own culture, the dominant culture, and the oppressive relationship between the two cultures. According to Torres (1996), a sense of ethnic identity is socially constructed from shared culture, religion, geography, and language that are often connected by strong loyalty and kinship as well as proximity. Several models of ethnic identity development have been proposed. Works by Cross (1978), Helms (1990), Kim (1981), Atkinson et al. (1983), and others share with the ego identity literature (Marcia, 1966, 1980) the idea that an achieved identity is the result of a crisis or awakening, which leads to a period of exploration or experimentation, and finally to a commitment or incorporation of one's ethnicity.

Although these models provide important conceptualizations, there has been relatively little research aimed at validating them, and much of the research has focused on a single ethnic group. In contrast, Phinney's (1990) research

Table 4.1 Stages of Racial/Cultural Identity Development

Authors	Stage 1	Stage 2	Stage 3	Stage 4	Stage 5
Atkinson, Morten, & Sue (1983)	Conformity	Dissonance	Resistance/ immersion		Synergetic articulation and awareness
Cross (1978)	Pre-encounter	Encounter	Immersion/ emersion	Internalization	Internalization/ commitment
Hardiman & Jackson (1992)	Naïve/no social consciousness	Acceptance	Resistance	Redefinition	Internalization
Helms (1994)	Contact	Disintegration	Reintegration	Pseudo-independence	Immersion/emersion autonomy
Kim (1981)	White-identified	Awakening to social-political consciousness	Redirection to Asian American consciousness	Incorporation	
Marcia (1966, 1980)	Identity diffusion or identity foreclosure	Identity crisis	Moratorium		Identity achievement
Milliones (1980) Phinney (1990)	Preconscious Unexamined ethnic identity —diffuse and/or foreclose	Confrontation	Ethnic identity search/ moratorium	Internalization	Integration Ethnic identity achievement
Sue & Sue (1999)	Conformity	Dissonance	Resistance/ immersion	Introspection	Integrative awareness

aimed at "developing and testing a model of ethnic identity development that is (1) theoretically based on Erikson's (1964, 1968) writings, (2) congruent both with Marcia's (1980) ego-identity statuses and with the models of ethnic identity in the literature, and (3) applicable across ethnic groups" (p. 63). As a result, she proposed the following three stages of development that many cultural groups experience as they struggle to define themselves: (1) unexamined ethnic identity, (2) ethnic identity search/moratorium, and (3) ethnic identity achievement.

Stage 1: Unexamined Ethnic Identity

According to Phinney (1993), stage 1 is characterized by a lack of interest or concern with ethnicity and a lack of exploration of ethnic issues. Several existing racial identity models suggest that minority subjects initially accept the values and attitudes of the majority culture, including internalized negative views and stereotypes of their own group that are held by the majority (i.e., white American societal values, standards, and preferences). Cross (1978) called this stage in which "the person's worldview is dominated by Euro-American determinants" (p. 17) *pre-encounter*. Likewise, Kim (1981) referred to this stage as *white-identified*, while Atkinson et al. (1983) described it as a *conformity stage*.

Apparent differences between the minority subject and whites are either not acknowledged, at least on the conscious level, or, if they do acknowledge their distinguishing physical and/or cultural characteristics, they view them as a source of shame. Described by Marcia in 1980, this stage of minority identity development might be compared to *identity foreclosure* (i.e., characterized by the absence of exploration of issues, accompanied by commitments based on attitudes and opinions adopted from others without question). Foreclosure can be negative or positive. For example, Phinney's (1993) studies found that a foreclosed ethnic identity does not necessarily imply white preference. "Adolescents whose parents have provided positive models of ethnic pride may be foreclosed in the sense of not having examined the issues for themselves, but may have a positive view of their own group" (p. 68).

Stage 2: Ethnic Identity Search/Moratorium

Phinney posited that stage 1 continues until adolescents encounter a situation that initiates stage 2, an ethnic identity search. With reference to ego identity, Erikson (1968) referred to this as the *identity crisis* or *moratorium*—"a necessary turning point, a crucial moment, when development must move one way or another, marshalling resources of growth, recovery, and further differentiation" (p. 16). Cross (1978) used the term *encounter* to describe this shocking personal or social event that temporarily dislodges the person from his or her old worldview, making the person receptive to a new interpretation of his or her identity. According to Phinney (1993), "it may be that an encounter experience is evident when individuals look back at the process of their own search, but that it is not clear at the time it happens" (p. 69).

Stage 2 of Phinney's model can be described as a time of experimentation and inquiry, which may include activities such as reading about various possibilities; taking relevant course work; talking with friends, parents, or others about the topic of interest; and actually trying out different life goals and lifestyles (Waterman, 1985). According to Cross (1978), this stage of *immersion/emersion* is characterized by an intense concern to clarify the personal implications of ethnicity and may be highly emotional. For example, Kim (1981) found that "included in this phase is anger and outrage directed toward white society. This occurs when [subjects] discover and allow themselves to feel some of the historical incidents of racism" (p. 149).

For Cross (1978), the process included "the tendency to denigrate white people and white culture while simultaneously deifying black people and black culture" (p. 17). Erikson (1964) acknowledged the intensity of this period and recognized the role of anger. He noted that a transitory "negative identity," or rejection of appropriate roles, may be a necessary precondition for a positive identity.

Stage 3: Ethnic Identity Achievement

According to Phinney (1993), "the ideal outcome of the identity process is an achieved identity, characterized by a clear, confident sense of one's own ethnicity" (p. 71). Individuals with an achieved ego identity have resolved uncertainties about their future direction and have made commitments that will guide future action (Marcia, 1980). Cross (1978), using the term *internalization* for this stage, described the following: "Tension, emotionality, and defensiveness are replaced by a calm, secure demeanor. Ideological flexibility, psychological openness, and self-confidence about one's blackness are evident" (p. 18).

During Phinney's stage 3, self-concept is positive, subjects feel good about who they are, they are comfortable blending aspects of their ethnic being, and they feel at home with themselves. They acknowledge a sense of self-fulfillment and pride with regard to cultural identity. All three of Phinney's stages of ethnic identity can be clearly and reliably distinguished, in contrast to some of the four or five ego statuses that have been described in the ethnic identity literature.

Racial and Cultural Autobiographies

As a transformative strategy, future leaders complete a cultural autobiography by naming the countries (if any), other than the United States, that they identify as a place of origin for themselves and their family. They make a list of at least five values that are important to their cultural/racial identity and rank order them from most important to least important. They also reflect upon particular family members' attitudes toward people who are culturally and ethnically different (e.g., white Americans, African Americans, Native Americans, Asian Americans, Hispanic/Latino Americans, gays/lesbians, disabled people, religious people, rich/poor people).

Adult learners share what they were encouraged to believe about people of other groups and identify what was and wasn't discussed growing up and why. They complete a list of sentence starters (i.e., As a boy/girl, I must . . .) and are encouraged to recall specific incidents in their life (five-year time blocks) that affected their thinking and/or feelings about people who are culturally or ethnically different from them. Future leaders then share what discoveries about their families stand out most and why.

Through the completion of cultural autobiographies, future leaders identify their ethnic/cultural group membership and reflect upon advice that has been handed down through their family by their ancestors (i.e., "family motto"). As adult learners reflected and reportedly grew in awareness of who they are today and who they want to be in the future, they also acknowledged an important connection to their past.

When recalling specific incidents in their life that affected their thinking and/or feelings about people who are different from them, many students realized that "my past is still so prevalent in my decisions about myself, my career, my family, and my interactions with others." Data analysis indicated that as future leaders perceived that they grew in an understanding of their cultural assumptions and presuppositions, they also related that they were engaging in perspective transformation.

> One of the many important things that I am learning from class is how I have been caught up in only my culture and have taken for granted all the wonderful cultures around me. There is so much more to learn and understand about other cultures that I really am beginning to feel like I have been blind for a great portion of my life.
>
> I've always known/heard that I'm a product of my past but never fully realized to what extent. Class readings, discussions, and activities are making me more aware of my family's influence on my thinking and actions. Now I want/ need to take some time to reflect deeply, to figure out what it actually is that I believe versus what my past tells me I should believe.

Being effective administrators means that we remember to consider the needs of all students and make no assumptions based on our own past experiences. This class is teaching us to recognize when those assumptions are at the core of our decision-making and to make amendments to those assumptions when necessary.

I am beginning to realize how much of a hypocrite I have been. I mean by me being a minority you would think that I would not fall into stereotyping other minorities. You would also think because of my education and experience that I would know better. This class is really making me take a deeper look at myself, at my past, and at people that are from different cultures. I am beginning to go beyond the surface and take the time to develop a true interest.

My Dad believes that all gays/lesbians are disgusting and if they don't get their lives together, they will not enter the "kingdom." He believes that all white Americans are nasty and are not to be trusted because they will steal your ideas and take credit. I realize now how important it is for me to identify and combat these negative "records" in my head. I must first be so conscious of these "tapes" in order to deal with them.

PREJUDICE REDUCTION WORKSHOPS

"Great possibilities for understanding and change open up when the problem of racism is framed as a matter of learning, unlearning, and relearning, rather than as a chronic, immutable fact of life" (Henze, Katz, Norte, Sather, & Walker, 2002, p. 23). Leaders for social justice, equity, and excellence are committed to lifelong learning and growth, to recognizing and eliminating prejudice and oppression, to increasing awareness, to facilitating change, and to building inclusive communities.

Preparation programs in educational leadership can foster such skills and empower adults to integrate new information into the knowledge they already have through participation in welcoming diversity workshops (see Sleeter, 1996). One example is the National Coalition Building Institute (NCBI) formula that relies on a unique blend of emotional healing, personal experience, and skills training methodologies to identify and reduce various forms of oppression and resolve intergroup conflict. Through a series of incremental, participatory activities, future leaders learn that guilt is the glue that holds prejudice in place, that every issue counts, that stories change attitudes, and that skills training leads to empowerment.

The NCBI workshops combine strategies from adult learning theory (i.e., self-directed learning, critical reflection, experiential learning, and learning to learn); transformative learning theory (i.e., centrality of experience, critical reflection, and rational discourse); and critical social theory (i.e., critical reflection and social action) in empowering individuals to become more effective leaders and allies on behalf of others. The objectives are as follows:

- To celebrate similarities and differences,
- To recognize the misinformation that people have learned about various groups,
- To identify and heal from internalized oppression—the discrimination members of an oppressed group target at themselves and each other,
- To claim pride in group identity,
- To understand the personal impact of discrimination through the narration of stories,
- To learn hands-on tools for dealing effectively with bigoted comments and behaviors. (NCBI, 2002)

By participating in a one-day interactive workshop, future leaders increase awareness of self, enabling them to be more reflective and effective advocates for others who take leadership in building inclusive communities in their workplaces, schools, and neighborhoods.

"We must keep in mind, however, that if the issues are not discussed, and the dialogue not begun, then urgent changes will not occur." This journal entry is typical of many of the adult learners' thoughts regarding discussions of race, diversity, social justice, and equity. The workshops helped future leaders acknowledge the difficulty and uneasiness of such conversations, while simultaneously encouraging them to commit to extended and repeated conversations. "It definitely made us aware of the need for action. It also caused us to acknowledge our own shortcomings. We can talk the talk, but can we walk the walk?"

> I think that it is important that we begin to step out of the comfort zone of being nice to each other and be honest, especially on issues of race. For me it is a learning process, and I would much rather learn here than as a principal.
>
> I have always been open to other people's opinions and viewpoints, but yesterday proved to me that perception and understanding are in constant evolution, changing and morphing with the relationship one has with others.
>
> The workshop discussions and activities helped me stretch myself and make some good discoveries. It really made me think about how groups of people have certain stereotypes and how other groups use and manipulate those very stereotypes.
>
> The world would be such a better place if people could just sit down and talk about their differences and voice their concerns. Some of the stories from my cohort members were very interesting and some were very sad. Darrell's story really made me emotional.

The last line of the previous quote relates to one story in particular that many of the students wrote about in their journals. During the diversity workshops, future leaders identify the information and misinformation they learned about other groups, they identify and express pride in the groups to which they belong, they learn how groups other than their own group experience mistreatment, and they learn about the personal impact of specific incidents of discrimination.

Darrell's story of being misidentified and profiled for crimes totally based on his racial heritage was extremely compelling. Darrell is a 31-year-old black male with dreadlocks who has been arrested twice because he "fit the profile." He is considering the possibility of cutting his hair in order to increase his job prospects as an assistant principal. Comments in adult learner journals included the following: "That is something I have never had to worry about," "I too was shocked that Darrell was arrested twice. He is such an upstanding citizen! He values other peoples' opinion of him. Surprisingly, he did not seem angry. That would be terribly difficult to get over," and "Wow! I never thought about what it might be like to be a black male in today's world. I'm exhausted."

Most would agree that one of the pinnacles of the workshop was the "black male" testimony. The first thought that comes to mind when beginning this learning experience is a paraphrase of a quote by Jesse Jackson. He made the comment that he knew it was becoming a dire situation for African Americans if and when he was walking alone at night and heard footsteps . . . and he turned around and would be relieved that it was a white person behind him. Many of us know that apprehension. Our society and our cultural perceptions have been shaped into the belief that the black male is violent, is untrustworthy, and is worthy to be feared. With these thoughts in place, I heard Darrell and Chad's story. To preface their accounts, I have never met two more admirable human beings—men whom I actually put on a pedestal. Their commitment to their careers and their family and their understanding of themselves place their maturity much further along than mine. Yet, it did not matter in our American society. Out from their mouths flowed stories and predicaments of racial type-casting and prejudicial treatment from the majority. Hardships that I had never faced emanated from their lives, and I shuddered for them and their role in this society.

DIVERSITY PRESENTATIONS AND PANELS

Fraser (1997) argued that what is needed for more fully democratic social institutions is cultural revaluation and political/economic redistribution. In order to understand how historical distrust affects present-day interactions, leaders for social justice, equity, and excellence need to learn about the origins of stereotypes and prejudices. Diversity panels challenge the presumption of entitlement and highlight the reality of institutionalized oppression. They bring to light the situations in which certain ways of being (i.e., having certain identities) are privileged in society, while others are marginalized.

By engaging in informed constructive discourse with people who are different from them, adult learners are forced to examine how power, privilege, and dominance are manifested and reinforced. Such discourse communities can provide the context in which future leaders recognize and experience the need to change, thereby relieving those identified as outsiders (i.e., the members of the excluded groups) from the responsibility of doing all the adapting. Diversity panels help adult learners grasp a thorough understanding of the dynamics of power relations, as well as the responsibilities that correspond with each position of power.

Specifically, those in the subordinate position have a responsibility to give voice to how decisions and actions affect them, and those in the dominant position have a responsibility to listen and respond (Norte, 2001). Delpit (1995) contended that both sides need to be able to listen and "that it is those with the most power, those in the majority, who must take the greater responsibility for initiating the process" (p. 46). Through participation in diversity panels, adult learners begin to differentiate between individual racism and institutional racism and come to the realization that everyone is an integral part of both the problem and the solution.

Together with others in the class who have chosen the same nonmonolithic group to study in depth, future leaders conduct the class on a given day. Students are expected to assign and distribute additional readings so that they can present the history of that group's educational experience in the United States (including the circumstances that brought or made them inhabitants of the United States), and how they were treated. The main objective is to help class members understand how the group has been treated in this country and how the history lives on and affects the present (e.g., philosophically, economically, politically, socially, and culturally).

Adult learners' presentations include (1) information regarding the values considered representative of the majority of people in that group, (2) a discussion of their schooling experiences, and (3) any other issues that they deem important (e.g., stereotypes, inequitable treatment, successful pedagogical strategies). Insights included the following:

> I know these presentations are very beneficial to my understanding of becoming "a needed change agent" but they surely cause me a lot of stress! Presenting these groups in isolation gives me a broader perspective on the same injustices going on today that have traveled through history with certain groups.
>
> To a certain degree, the information that I heard was painful. History is becoming more and more insufferable. My ancestors did this damage to these people. The effect is still being felt today. I have a responsibility to help correct the situation. I need to research, read, dig for information in all aspects of other races to help understand how I will be able to make the greatest impact as an administrator.

> I am beginning to realize how much of a hypocrite I have been. I mean by me being a minority you would think that I would not fall into stereotyping other minorities. You would also think because of my education and experience that I would know better. This class is really making me take a deeper look at people that are from different cultures. I am beginning to go beyond the surface and take the time to develop a true interest. I have never taken the time to look at Hispanic-Americans individually. I would always put them into one group.

As part of this particular class, future leaders also facilitate a one-hour panel presentation from at least three people from the nonmonolithic group being studied that day. Panel members introduce themselves, engage in a sharing of their educational experiences, and participate in an informal question and answer session with all members of the cohort. Cultural values, lessons taught, schooling experiences, and misperceptions experienced are discussed. Panel members are also asked for suggestions in working more effectively with students from all cultures. Findings indicate an increase in awareness and acknowledgment as future leaders reflect on what they heard, learned, and felt during the diversity panels.

> I was astonished at the terrified feelings one of the panel members shared about riding the bus with American children of different cultural backgrounds than herself. This helped me to realize that as an administrator it is important that I make all children and staff feel safe at school and comfortable so their learning environment can be as productive as possible.
>
> At the close of the class, during the panel I really began to understand this problem. I feel for every adult and child that may be homeless. I began to think about my own students. I wonder if any of them are homeless. I wonder if they are, what can I do about it, how can I tell, and how do I know? I finally resolved in my mind that it is important to treat students with respect. It is even more important to nurture every child. When children know you care, they trust you. Even if they do not disclose information, they should always know that you believe in them and their potential to be successful.
>
> Today's class was one that was most insightful to me. I think back to what Carla stated when she said she has been referred to as Gal, Nigga, and other derogatory remarks in her hometown. This was surprising to me, not because this is supposed to be the "new age," but simply for the reason that people still have the audacity to do and say things to your face. I could really hear the hurt in her voice.

CONCLUSION

Engaging in the critical self-reflection that may lead to change in perspective is, in itself, a process that requires self-awareness, planning, skill, support, and discourse with others. In order to really bridge theory and practice, transformative learning is needed. As future leaders for social justice, equity, and excellence grow in an awareness of self through critical reflection, the next andragogical step in this process involves an increase in the acknowledgment of others through rational discourse. Chapter 5 describes three such discourse procedures designed to ensure openness, respect, and equal participation. Through interviewing, listening, and engaging others, adult learners can grow in a much deeper understanding of past, present, and future educational issues.

CRITICAL QUESTIONS

1. *Name three concrete ways that a principal could help his or her teachers and staff develop as critically reflective educators? What would be the purpose and intended outcomes?*
2. *What resources are currently available in your school, district, community, and state that actively promote diversity awareness and prejudice reduction issues? Be sure to research programs provided to health care workers, law enforcement, and social agencies.*
3. *How might a principal utilize cultural autobiographies and biographies within the context of monthly faculty meetings? What role does rational discourse play in these monthly meetings? Why? How?*

REFERENCES

Adams, G. R., Gullotta, T. P., & Montemayor, R. (1992). *Adolescent identity formation*. Thousand Oaks, CA: Sage.

Arce, C. (1981). A reconsideration of Chicano culture and identity. *Daedalus, 110*(2), 177–192.

Atkinson, D., Morten, G., & Sue, D. W. (1983). *Counseling American minorities*. Dubuque, IA: Wm. C. Brown.

Banks, J. (1994). *Multiethnic education: Theory and practice*. Needham Heights, MA: Allyn & Bacon.

Berzonsky, M. D., & Kuk, L. S. (2000). Identity status, identify processing style and the transition to University. *Journal of Adolescent Research, 15*(1), 81–98.

Brookfield, S. D. (1995). Adult learning: An overview. In A. Tuinjman (Ed.), *International encyclopedia of education*. Oxford, UK: Pergamon.

Brown, S., Parham, T., & Yonker, R. (1996). Influence of a cross-cultural training course on racial identity attitudes of White women and men: Preliminary perspectives. *Journal of Counseling & Development, 74*, 510–516.

Carter, R. T. (1997). Is white a race?: Expressions of white racial identity. In M. Fine, L. Weiss, L. C. Powell, & L. Mun Wond (Eds.), *Off white: Readings on race, power, and society* (pp.198–209). New York, NY: Routledge.

Cass, V. C. (1979). Homosexual identity formation: A theoretical model. *Journal of Homosexuality, 4,* 219–235.

Chavez, A. F., & Guido-DiBrito, F. (1999). Racial and ethnic identity and development. *New Directions for Adult and Continuing Education, 84,* 39–49.

Coleman, P., & Deutsch, M. (1995). The mediation of interethnic conflict in schools. In W. Hawley & A. Jackson (Eds.), *Toward a common destiny: Improving race and ethnic relations in America* (pp. 371–396). San Francisco, CA: Jossey-Bass.

Cranton, P. (1994). *Understanding and promoting transformative learning: A guide for educators of adults.* San Francisco, CA: Jossey-Bass.

Cross, W. E. (1978). The Thomas and Cross models of psychological nigrescence: A literature review. *Journal of Black Psychology, 4,* 13–31.

Cross, W. E. (1994). Nigrescence theory: Historical and explanatory notes. *Journal of Vocational Behavior, 44,* 119–123.

Cross, W. E. (1995). In search of blackness and afrocentricity: The psychology of black identity change. In H. W. Harris, H. C. Blue, & E. E. H. Griffith (Eds.), *Racial and ethnic identity: Psychological development and creative expression* (pp. 53–72). New York, NY: Routledge.

Delpit, L. (1995). *Other people's children: Cultural conflict in the classroom.* New York, NY: New Press.

Dewey, J. (1910). *How we think.* Boston, MA: Heath.

Erikson, E. (1959/1980). *Identity and the life cycle.* New York, NY: Norton.

Erikson, E. (1964). *Insight and responsibility.* New York, NY: Norton.

Erikson, E. (1968). *Identity: Youth and crisis.* New York, NY: Norton.

Fraser, N. (1997). *Justice interrupts: Critical reflections on the "postsocialist" condition.* New York, NY: Routledge.

Freire, P. (1970/1990/ 1992). *Pedagogy of the oppressed.* New York, NY: Seabury.

Garrett, J. T., & Walking Stick Garrett, M. (1994). The path of good medicine: Understanding and counseling Native American Indians. *Journal of Multicultural Counseling and Development, 22,* 134–144.

Gibbs, J. T. (1987). Identity and marginality: Issues in the treatment of biracial adolescents. *American Journal of Orthopsychiatry, 57,* 265–278.

Hardiman, R., & Jackson, B. W. (1992). Racial identity development: Understanding racial dynamics in college classrooms and on campus. *New Directions for Teaching and Learning, 52,* 21–37.

Helms, J. E. (1990). *Black and white racial identity: Theory, research and practice.* New York, NY: Greenwood.

Helms, J. E. (1993). *Black and white racial identity: Theory, research and practice.* Westport, CT: Praeger.

Helms, J. E. (1994). Racial identity in the school environment. In P. Pedersen & J. C. Carey (Eds.), *Multicultural counseling in schools* (pp. 19–37). Boston, MA: Allyn and Bacon.

Helms, J. E. (1995). An update on Helm's white and people of color racial identity models. In J. G. Ponterotto, J. M. Casas, L. A. Suzuki, & C. M. Alexander (Eds.), *Handbook of multicultural counseling* (pp. 181–191). Thousand Oaks, CA: Sage.

Henze, R., Katz, A., Norte, E., Sather, S., & Walker, E. (2002). *Leading for diversity: How school leaders promote positive interethnic relations.* Thousand Oaks, CA: Corwin.

Horse, P. G. (2001). Reflections on American Indian identity. In C. L. Wijeye-singhe & B. W. Jackson (Eds.), *New perspectives on racial identity development* (pp. 91–107). New York, NY: New York University.

Jackson, B. (1975). Black identity development. In L. Goldschick & B. Persky (Eds.), *Urban social educational issues.* Dubuque, IA: Kendall-Hunt.

Katz, J. H. (1989). The challenge of diversity. In C. Woolbright (Ed.), *College unions at work, Monograph no. 11* (pp. 1–17). Bloomington, IN: Association of College Unions-International.

Kim, J. (1981). *The process of Asian-American identity development. A study of Japanese American women's perceptions of their struggle to achieve positive identities.* Unpublished doctoral dissertation, University of Massachusetts, Amherst.

Larrivee, B. (2000). Transforming teaching practice: Becoming the critically reflective teacher. *Reflective Practice, 1*(3), 293–307.

Lee, S. R. (1988). *Self-concept correlates of Asian American cultural identity attitudes.* Unpublished doctoral dissertation. University of Maryland, College Park.

Marcia, J. (1966). Development and validation of ego-identity status. *Journal of Personality and Social Psychology, 3,* 551–558.

Marcia, J. (1980). Identity in adolescence. In J. Adelson (Ed.), *Handbook of adolescent psychology* (pp. 159–187). New York, NY: Wiley.

Marcia, J., Waterman, A., Matteson, D., Archer, S., & Orlofsky, J. (1994). *Ego identity: A handbook of psychosocial research.* New York, NY: Springer-Verlag.

Mezirow, J. (1991). *Transformative dimensions of adult learning.* San Francisco, CA: Jossey-Bass.

Miller, J. (1998). Autobiography as a queer curriculum practice. In W. E. Pinar (Ed.), *Queer theory in education* (pp. 365–373). Mahwah, NJ: Lawrence Erlbaum.

Milliones, J. (1980). Construction of a Black consciousness measure: Psychotherapeutic implications. Psychotherapy: Theory, Research & Practice, 17(2), 175–182.

National Coalition Building Institute (NCBI). (2002). Retrieved from http://ncbi.org/.

Norte, E. (2001). Structures beneath the skin: How school leaders use their power and authority to create institutional opportunities for developing positive interethnic communities. *Journal of Negro Education, 68*(4), 466–485.

O'Hearn, C. C. (1998). *Half and half: Writers growing up biracial and bicultural.* New York, NY: Pantheon Books.

Parham, T. (1989). Cycles of psychological nigrescence. *The Counseling Psychologist, 17*(2), 187–226.

Parham, T., & Helms, J. (1981). The influence of Black students' racial identity attitudes on preferences for counselor's race. *Journal of Counseling Psychology, 28,* 250–257.

Phinney, J. (1990). Ethnic identity in adolescents and adults: review of research. *Psychological Bulletin, 108*, 499–514.

Phinney, J. (1993). A three-stage model of ethnic identity development in adolescence. In M. E. Bernal & G. P. Knight (Eds.), *Ethnic identity: Formation and transmission among Hispanics and other minorities* (pp. 61–79). Albany, NY: State University of New York.

Phinney, J., Cantu, C., & Kurtz, D. (1997). Ethnic and American identity as predictors of self-esteem among African American, Latino, and white adolescents. *Journal of Youth and Adolescence, 26*, 165–185.

Piaget, J. (1952). *The origins of intelligence in children.* New York, NY: International Universities.

Ponterotto, J., & Pedersen, P. (1993). *Preventing prejudice: A guide for counselors and educators.* Thousand Oaks, CA: Sage.

Schon, D. (1987). *Educating the reflective practitioner.* San Francisco, CA: Jossey-Bass.

Sleeter, C. (1996). *Multicultural education as social activism.* Albany, NY: State University of New York.

Sue, D. W., & Sue, D. (1999). *Counseling the culturally different: Theory and practice* (3rd ed.). New York, NY: John Wiley & sons.

Tajfel, H. (1978). *The social psychology of minorities.* New York, NY: Minority Rights Group.

Torres, V. (1996, March). *Empirical studies in Latino/Latina ethnic identity.* Paper presented at the National Association of Student Personnel Administrators National Conference, Baltimore, MD.

Waterman, A. (1985). Identity in the context of adolescent psychology. In A. Waterman (Ed.), *Identity in adolescence: Process and contents,* (pp. 5–24). San Francisco, CA: Jossey-Bass.

York, D. (1994). *Cross-cultural training programs.* Westport, CN: Bergin & Garvey.

Chapter 5

Acknowledgment of Others through Rational Discourse

INTRODUCTION

Rational discourse involves a commitment to extended and repeated conversations that evolve over time into a culture of careful listening and cautious openness to new perspectives, not shared understanding in the sense of consensus, but rather deeper and richer understandings of our own biases as well as where our colleagues are coming from on particular issues and how each of us differently constructs those issues. Educational psychologist Jerome Bruner (1988) suggested that people are able to process complex information much more easily when it comes in narrative form. Given this, participation in extended and repeated discourse about social justice, equity, and excellence can provide unique opportunities for learner growth, transformation, and empowerment.

> As we struggle to understand how issues of race and ethnicity affect the educational experiences for all students, we must work to overcome our prejudices by listening carefully to those whose backgrounds, perspectives, and understandings differ from our own. We must examine popular assumptions as well as the politically correct stereotypes that educators often use to explain what is happening in today's multicultural society and its increasingly ethnically heterogeneous schools. Engaging in socially just leadership requires us to maintain an open conversation, to examine and reexamine our perceptions and those of others, constantly looking beneath the surface and seeking alternative explanations and ways of understanding. (Shields, Larocque, & Oberg, 2002, p. 134)

Rational discourse validates meaning by assessing reasons. It involves weighing the supporting evidence, examining alternative perspectives, and critically assessing assumptions. Through participation in rational discourse processes, many future leaders are able to "find their voice" in constructive dialogue with others (a prerequisite for full free participation). According to Senge (1990), "The discipline of mental models starts with turning the mirror inward; learning to unearth our internal pictures of the world, to bring them to the surface and hold them rigorously to scrutiny" (p. 9). Analysis of the data confirmed adult learners' perceived ability to carry on "learningful conversations that balance inquiry and advocacy, where people expose their own thinking effectively and make that thinking open to the influence of others" (Senge, 1990, p. 9).

Establishing a dialogic context, however, can be complicated, difficult, and frightening for students and professors alike. Unlike conversation in which genial cooperation prevails, dialogue actually aims at disequilibrium in which "each argument evokes a counterargument that pushes itself beyond the other and pushes the other beyond itself" (Lipman, 1991, p. 232). Dialogue focuses more on inquiry and increasing understanding and tends to be more exploratory and questioning than conversation. Acknowledgment is a necessary step in linking awareness to action.

Through rational discourse, awareness is validated, refined, and focused, and motives leading to social action are cultivated.

Rational discourse can be stimulated through an array of techniques, including class discussions, "provocative declaratives" (see Vavrus, 2002), critical incidents (see Flanagan, 1954; Tripp, 1993), controversial readings, and/or structured group activities. Believing that no curriculum is neutral, Freire's pedagogy gives priority to the use of dialogue. The use of questions and a dialogic teaching approach gives the learners more control over their own experience; it allows them to become the teachers of their own experience and culture and to apply those insights to their own leadership practice.

In this chapter, three andragogical discourse procedures are described that help ensure openness, respect, and equal participation (Educational Leadership Constituent Council (ELCC) dimension of Understanding): (1) past: conducting oral life histories, (2) present: engaging in cross-cultural interviews, and (3) future: exploring educational plunges.

ACKNOWLEDGING THE PAST THROUGH ORAL LIFE HISTORIES

We need to understand what currently exists before we can begin to understand what *should* exist (Giroux, 1992). Without history, people make decisions based on a truncated knowledge base. Without history, people fail to understand how current societal tensions have emerged from events and trends of the past. In 1938, Dewey noted:

> The nature of the issues cannot be understood save as we know they came about. The institutions and customs that exist in the present and that gave rise to present social ills and dislocations did not arise overnight. They have a long history behind them. Attempts to deal with them simply on the basis of what is obvious in the present are bound to result in adoption of superficial measures which in the end will only render existing problems more acute and more difficult to solve. (p. 77)

In preparing leaders for social justice, equity, and excellence, principal preparation programs need to teach an accurate history of schooling in this country, including the deeply rooted systematic nature of the inequities reproduced daily. By providing a retrospective, contemporary, and prospective examination of the social, cultural, political, economic, and philosophical contexts from which the current issues that affect schools and schooling have evolved, professors can help adult learners begin to acknowledge and question the origins of educational policies and practices. In other words, "By making conventional views of U.S. history and educational practices problematic, transformation resists White assimilationist conceptions of social change in favor of concern over social justice and equity" (Vavrus, 2002, p. 7).

Life histories are a means of fostering consciousness-raising and transformative experiential learning. Life histories seek to "examine and analyze the subjective experience of individuals and their constructions of the social world" (Jones, 1983, p. 147). By interviewing a person who is over the age of fifty-five and who attended school in the United States, future leaders enter vicariously into those same experiences and grow in their personal awareness of the historical context of contemporary education.

Adult learners listen as the interviewees share their educational story, including where they attended school, what type of schools they attended, and the setting of these schools. Interviewees are asked to describe the climate and culture of their schools, the structure and format of their courses, and the expectations/requirements of the times. Adult learners are instructed to probe the interviewees' memories regarding the major political, social, philosophical, and economic events during the interviewees' school years (e.g., the Depression, World War II, communism, atomic bomb, *Sputnik*, SATs, desegregation, vocational education), and how these happenings affected their education and career path (e.g., Did they attend high school/college?

What were their classes preparing them for? What was the ideology of the times? What were the societal issues? Who was involved with the school and why?). Students are then expected to synthesize and relate their experiential knowledge to the course material.

By listening to another's story, future leaders garner practical knowledge in how language dehumanizes by objectifying, how entitlement is manifested by oppression, and how ignorance is preserved by "omissions, distortions and fallacious assumptions being taught in school" (Lindsey, Robins, & Terrell, 1999, p. 106). As adult learners reportedly grow in their understanding of how current societal tensions have emerged from events and trends of the past, so too do their perceived consciousness and acknowledgment of what previous generations have experienced. They are "amazed at how many of the educational issues and problems from 'back in the day' are still so prevalent and unresolved today."

Another student added, "I tend to think that until we can look boldly at the real issues plaguing our profession, we will operate in the same fashion as our predecessors." Comments such as these could be found throughout future leaders' journal entries. They acknowledge that "older people are our best connections to the past," that "the historical information shared was directly related to the readings and our future as leaders," and that "oral histories are an enjoyable, rich way of sharing information that seems dull on paper."

A great way to honor my dad, and see how he lived out many of the issues in education we discussed and read about.

This class really opened my eyes to the importance of having a solid foundation of the history of the United States. I have begun to gain a greater sense of inquiry about how the events of the past influence the decisions made today. The interview made me realize the reactive nature of education in comparison to societal happenings. I am starting to take a more holistic view of education, which is what I will have to do as an administrator.

I am not usually a history person but the facts are so very informative and hauntingly relevant still today. How do you counteract or fight against the very structure and system that our country's educational foundation was built upon?

For the historical interview, I interviewed my father who is ninety-one years old. It was an interesting experience to find out new things about him, but even more interesting was to view his personal history as a reflection of national history. I tended to think of my family's history as somehow "out of touch" and idiosyncratic. Some of my father's comments were things I'd heard before, but thought of as his own oddball, sarcastic ideas. In researching the history, his comments make a lot more sense now.

ACKNOWLEDGING THE PRESENT THROUGH CROSS-CULTURAL INTERVIEWS

Henze et al. (2002) noted that "it is a recipe for conflict to act in the world based on the assumption that we have an objective view of it. In contrast, to assume that we each have a valid view of the world and have something to learn from each other's perspectives is the basis for mutual respect and appreciation" (p. 20). Because we, as a species, are apparently wired to listen to, engage in, and remember stories much better than we do with nonnarrative discourses (Viadero, 1990), providing future leaders with a learning opportunity to interact with someone from another ethnic, socioeconomic, religious, or sexual orientation background is a useful strategy in supporting cross-cultural development and respect.

In fact, critical social theory calls for the legitimization of counter-narratives that uncover various perspectives related to race, gender, and poverty. As such, this approach fosters positive relations and requires a greater depth of knowledge, introspection, and sincere intent than may be found in status quo, or even politically correct reactions.

Cross-cultural interviews involve a one-on-one encounter with an individual who is different from the adult learner in ethnicity/race. The purpose is to help future leaders develop a greater understanding of alternative worldviews, to increase their comfort in discussing differences and similarities, and to better appreciate the educational experiences of someone from a different background. Adult learners select an individual who is eighteen years of age or older, who attended school in the United States, who is different from themselves in ethnicity/race, and someone who will push their comfort zone (sample questions provided by the instructor query interviewees' cultural values, importance of education, experiences of racism, etc.).

The face-to-face interviews are conducted in a mutually agreed-upon safe, private place. In an effort to build rapport, adult learners are instructed to engage in some self-disclosure so that the interview is not totally one-sided. For example, future leaders might talk about what they have been learning about themselves in class, as well as any new understandings they have gained about oppression and discrimination.

In their follow-up reflection paper, students complete a "Subjective I" paper. After dividing their paper into three columns, in the first column, adult learners fully describe the cross-cultural interaction in which they were involved. They break this description into segments that reflect the nature and flow of the interaction—describing the experience, giving an overview of the interviewee (e.g., ethnicity/race, family background, salient attitudes/beliefs/experiences, cultural values, racial identity development, schooling details), and summarizing the central issues concerning the interviewee's educational experience.

In the middle, narrow column, next to each segment, they then identify the "Subjective I" that was operating at the time. In the third column, students comment on ways in which each "Subjective I" influenced the situation—they describe their emotional response to the cross-cultural interview, along with the insights/lessons gained. (See appendix 5.A for an example of the Cross-Cultural Interview "Guide.") At the end, future leaders write a paragraph or two in which they reflect upon the experience of doing this exercise and the insights they obtained in the process (e.g., What was of value to you? What did you learn in general? about cross-cultural interviewing? new understandings about self or "other"? What are your cultural insights? What are your insights into cross-cultural interactions/interviewing/education?).

By engaging in informed constructive discourse with people who are different from them, adult learners were forced to examine how power, privilege, and dominance are manifested and reinforced. Such discourse communities provided the context in which many of the future leaders reportedly began to recognize and experience the need to change, thereby relieving those identified as outsiders (i.e., the members of the excluded groups), from the responsibility of doing all the adapting.

> I have the power to make a difference. I now realize that I also have the responsibility to do that. I must listen and respond. I want to initiate the process no matter how difficult. I want to be a good ally and a great leader who makes a difference for all.
>
> I think that it is important that we begin to step out of the comfort zone of being nice to each other and be honest, especially on issues of race. For me it is a learning process, and I would much rather learn here than as a principal.
>
> I have always been open to other people's opinions and viewpoints, but yesterday proved to me that perception and understanding are in constant evolution, changing and morphing with the relationship one has with others.

When describing their emotional response to the cross-cultural interview, students described it as a "tough but quite valuable assignment." It "pushed my boundaries, forced me to go beyond what I am familiar with, helped me see my blind spots, tested the amount of fortitude that I had within myself, and made me have to stretch myself so thin I thought I was going to have to go into therapy just to debrief." Others concurred:

> Loved it and hated it. Loved it because it forced me to recognize my own biases, misconceptions, and ignorance. Hated it for the same reason. Definitely the most memorable (and probably the most valuable) experience this entire semester.

It is fascinating to me that with the three papers I have written for this class that the same lesson has come through as the lesson learned—don't judge, don't believe the stereotypes, treat children and adults as individuals!

It was a real challenge, thus, really rewarding—a great experience. It was a chance for me to risk a little and to deepen a friendship that wasn't as developed as I thought.

I believe by examining issues from various perspectives we get a much truer image of the reality. What I got from this cross-cultural interview was the great intellectual challenge of making valid decisions based on holistic views.

ACKNOWLEDGING THE FUTURE THROUGH EDUCATIONAL PLUNGES

"The worldviews of many in our society exist in protected cocoons. These individuals have never had to make an adjustment from home life to public life, as their public lives and the institutions they have encountered merely reflect a 'reality' these individuals have been schooled in since birth" (Delpit, 1995, p. 74). From the critical theorist's perspective that we are all cocooned in one way or another, the purpose of the educational plunge is to help future leaders emerge from their cocoons, to set the stage for questioning "accepted educational practices" and for openly challenging the "status quo." The contrast between *other* ways of education and *their* way of schooling raises adult awareness that *their* way is not the only normal way and that *their* beliefs and assumptions are not universally shared.

By encouraging future leaders to travel somewhat outside their usual milieu, they are made to experience this realization more directly. Making the familiar strange makes adults reflect on their own social environment in a new way. The jolting experience of culture shock results in an increased appreciation of how their social environment shapes their most basic attitudes, beliefs, and behaviors. Educational plunges honor the constructs of transformative learning theory—the centrality of experience, the need for critical reflection, and the necessity of rational discourse throughout the learning process.

Visits to "other" educational settings illustrate that there are other viable ways to operate schools and to teach effectively and that basic assumptions can differ in remarkable ways. That is, educators can often view the "way things are" as the "only way things can be." Educational plunges provide a "context change" (Cranton, 1992); they force the ground to shift—that which is accepted as "normal" or "unchangeable" is forced to be examined through a new lens.

Based on their own self-assessment regarding level of experience, comfort, awareness, and knowledge, future leaders decide which activity would be most beneficial to them in terms of furthering their awareness. The goal is for adult learners to select an activity that will challenge them to move beyond their present level of comfort, knowledge, and awareness and yet not be so uncomfortable or threatening that they are unable to be open to the "minority experience." This direct contact plunge involves a cross-cultural encounter "up close and personal." Future leaders are instructed to visit an educational setting unlike any they've experienced (e.g., private, Catholic, charter, magnet, single-sex schools, religious institutions, training centers, literacy councils, ESL programs, prisons or tutoring services, poor urban or wealthy academies, Head Start to college level, traditional, alternative, vocational, or technical).

Criteria for a plunge are (1) the majority of the people there are from the focal group, (2) adult learners are on the educational turf of the focal group, (3) plunge is a type of experience adult learners have never had before, (4) the plunge takes place after the course begins (no credit for past experience), (5) the plunge lasts at least one hour, (6) the plunge pushes adults' "comfort zone," and (7) future leaders have face-to-face interaction with people from the focal group.

In their follow-up reflection paper, adult learners describe the experience; their reasons for selecting the experience; their assumptions and biases about the focal community members and how they were challenged by this experience (if they were); their emotional response to the plunge (e.g., before, during, and after such as fear, anxiety, surprise, shock, disturbed, comfort/ discomfort, joy, and elation); the value of the experience (e.g., lessons, understandings, changes); and the relationship of experience to specific class readings and discussions, including implications for them as educational leaders for social justice, equity, and excellence.

> Loved this. By far, produced the most meaningful insight for me personally.
>
> An eye-opening day. I appreciate the assignment because it gave me an opportunity to go someplace I would not have gone otherwise.
>
> I'm really glad we were assigned this activity. I have always wondered what adult ESL classes look and feel like. This assignment gave me an excuse to go. Wow! I will never be the same as a result. My admiration for people who don't speak English has increased 100%. I will never look at them the same. This experience has given me some first-hand knowledge that I can share with others who are ignorant or prejudiced.

CONCLUSION

If future educational leaders have engaged in self-directed learning, critical reflection, and rational discourse regarding their underlying assumptions about practice, the next logical step is to integrate these assumptions into an informed theory of practice. Chapter 6 describes andragogical strategies that lead adult learners to action for equity through policy praxis.

CRITICAL QUESTIONS

1. *How might a principal help change the tenor of his or her faculty lounge from one of unproductive negativity and gossip to one of productive, proactive discourse around issues of equity and excellence? Is it realistic? Why/why not? Is it desirable? Why/why not?*

2. *What are the tenets of Professional Learning Communities (PLCs) and what role does rational discourse play in them? How? Why do some PLCs work better than others? What factors are necessary for rational discourse to take place, and how are these nurtured?*

3. *Name three concrete ways that a principal might help his or her teachers, staff members, parents, and students make a paradigm shift from looking out for self to taking care of others.*

REFERENCES

Bruner, J. (1988). Research currents: Life as narrative. *Language Arts, 65*(6), 574–583.

Cranton, P. (1992). *Working with adult learners.* Toronto, Canada: Wall & Emerson.

Delpit, L. (1995). *Other people's children: Cultural conflict in the classroom.* New York, NY: New Press.

Dewey, J. (1938). *Experience and education.* New York, NY: Simon and Schuster.

Flanagan, J. C. (1954). The critical incident technique. *Psychological Bulletin, 51,* 4.

Giroux, H. (1992). *Border crossings: Cultural workers and the politics of education.* New York, NY: Routledge.

Henze, R., Katz, A., Norte, E., Sather, S., & Walker, E. (2002). *Leading for diversity: How school leaders promote positive interethnic relations.* Thousand Oaks, CA: Corwin.

Jones, M. C. (1983). *Novelist as biographer: The truth of art, the lies of biography.* Unpublished doctoral dissertation, Northwestern University.

Lindsey, R., Robins, K., & Terrell, R. (1999). *Cultural proficiency: A manual for school leaders.* Thousand Oaks, CA: Corwin.

Lipman, M. (1991). *Thinking in education.* Cambridge, MA: Cambridge University.

Senge, P. (1990). *The fifth discipline: The art & practice of the learning organization.* New York, NY: Doubleday.

Shields, C., Larocque, L., & Oberg, S. (2002). A dialogue about race and ethnicity in education: Struggling to understand issues in cross-cultural leadership. *Journal of School Leadership, 12*(2), 116–137.

Tripp, D. (1993). *Critical incidents in teaching: Developing professional judgment.* New York, NY: Routledge.

Vavrus, M. (2002). *Transforming the multicultural education of teachers: Theory, research and practice.* New York, NY: Teachers College.

Viadero, D. (1990, March 28). Teacher educators turn to case-study method. *Education Week, 1*, 18–19.

APPENDIX 5.A

Cross-Cultural Interview "Guide"

1 Briefly describe your family of origin, including ethnicity/race; composition; generation in the United States; reason for immigration (if relevant); which region of the United States your family members have lived in; occupations of grandparents, parents, and siblings; authority structure; how names are chosen, and so forth.

2 What values do you see as of great importance in your culture? How are values of mainstream U.S. culture different from those of your culture? What kinds of conflicts or stress has this caused you or your family?

3 What does "family" mean to you? Do you think your meaning is different from mainstream people in the United States? If so, how?

4 What does "success" mean in your culture? What were you taught about how to be successful?

5 What place does education play in your culture? Describe *your* schooling experience.

6 What are the roles of grandparents, parents, and children in your culture? Men and women?

7 What other cultural groups are/were most and least respected in your family of origin? For what reasons? What place does religion play in your family?

8 When was the first time that you became aware that you were black, white, brown, and so forth? What were the circumstances surrounding this incident? How did you feel? What impact did the incident have on you?

9 What was it like to grow up as a black female, white male, Latino girl, Asian man, and so forth in the United States?

10 How did you first come to understand that racism existed. What happened? What were your feelings then? What are they now? What did you learn from this early experience? How does racism affect you now?

11 How were race-related issues handled in your family? Did your parents/ guardians discuss race and/or race-related issues? If so, what types of

things were discussed? What was your parent's main advice to you about people of other races?

12 As a child and adolescent what were the racial or ethnic backgrounds of your friends?

13 Describe your interactions with people who are racially or ethnically similar to you and with those who are racially different from you.

14 What is the nicest/meanest, most helpful/hurtful thing anyone of another race ever said or did to you or someone close to you? What did you feel? What did you do?

15 How much of a concern would it be to your family if you go for help outside of the family?

16 What other things do you think I need to know about your culture so that I can be a better helper? What are common problems or sources of stress experienced by members of your group in schools? What are common misperceptions experienced by members of your culture?

17 What suggestions would you make to school teachers and administrators working effectively with kids/families?

Chapter 6

Action for Equity through Policy Praxis

INTRODUCTION

Praxis is a Greek word that means moving back and forth in a critical way between reflecting and acting on the world. Because reflection alone does not produce change, Freire (1970) advocated for the necessity of action based on reflection. Policy praxis involves inductive and deductive forms of reasoning. It also involves dialogue as social process with the objective of "dismantling oppressive structures and mechanisms prevalent both in education and society" (Freire & Macedo, 1995, p. 383).

Critical, transformative leaders enter and remain in education not to carry on business as usual but to work for social change and social justice (Ayers, Hunt, & Quinn, 1998; Cochran-Smith, 1998; Oakes & Lipton, 1999). Unfortunately, Rapp et al. (2001) found that 90 percent of educational leaders, both practitioners and professors, remained wedded to what Scott and Hart (1979) call *technical drifting*—a commitment to emphasize and act upon the technical components of one's work above the moral.

Technical drifters fail to validate the cultural, intellectual, and emotional identities of people from underrepresented groups, they avoid situations where their values (e.g., sexist, racist, classist, homophobic), leadership styles, and professional goals are challenged and dismantled, and they use their positions of power to formally and informally reaffirm their own professional choices.

Given this disturbing reality, courageous, transformative leadership is needed. According to Mezirow (1990), "Every adult educator has the responsibility for fostering critical self-reflection and helping learners plan to take action" (p. 357). Educational activists need to be attuned to the complexities of changing demographics and must be willing "to engage in and facilitate critical and constructive inquiry" (Sirontnik & Kimball, 1996, p. 187).

In an effort to develop the risk-taking, political, and human relations skills necessary to do this, leadership preparation programs need to expose future leaders to critical social theory and its influence on the purposes of schooling. This recommendation is consistent with Astin's (1993) finding that on campuses where faculty stated that a goal of their institution was to promote student social activism, more positive change was seen in student interest and valuing of activism.

Transformative learning theory leads to a new way of seeing. This in turn leads to some kind of action. Dunn (1987) suggested that there is an ontological link between personal beliefs and public behaviors; that the true test of connection between personal understandings and individual and/or collective public responsibility is the degree to which any of the talk we engage in about social justice prompts us to a different kind of activism.

People seeking to shift the balance of power must understand their own distinctive role in ending oppression. "For entitled people (dominant group members), their role requires a moral choice to assume personal responsibility and to take personal initiative. For oppressed people (nondominant group members), their role is to recognize oppression and to commit themselves to self-determination" (Lindsey, Robins, & Terrell, 1999, p. 96).

If future educational leaders have engaged in self-directed learning, critical reflection, and rational discourse regarding their underlying assumptions about practice, the next logical step is to integrate these assumptions into an informed theory of practice (i.e., social action). Trueba (1999) explained:

> The praxis that accompanies a pedagogy of hope is clearly a conscious detachment from 'whiteness' and from a rigid, dogmatic, and monolithic defense of a Western or North American way of life, schooling codes, and interactional patterns. A simple change of technique and a paternalistic response to 'these poor immigrant children' [or to other children of color ill served by public education] will definitely not do. Educators who are serious about their praxis and committed to a pedagogy of hope must be prepared to take a long and hazardous psychological trip into lands and minds unknown before . . . this praxis is incompatible with despair, negligence, disrespect, and racism. (p. 161)

Increasing adult learner awareness of how we are all agents of change as educators is a vital part of development. Helping future leaders see how this new awareness and acknowledgment can be focused and acted upon in a meaningful way in real schools and in real communities is as critically important. Community-based learning or service learning is one such strategy that has the potential to deepen understanding, to strengthen skills, and to promote civic responsibility.

In this chapter, three andragogical strategies for helping future leaders set and implement goals in terms of behaviors, boundaries, alternatives, and consequences are offered (i.e., activist action plans, social agency site visits, and school/district equity audits). In learning about themselves and others, adults in principal preparation programs are invited to think independently, to observe, to experience, to reflect, to learn, and to dialogue. Challenging them to act for equity (ELCC dimension of Capability) is the next step.

ACTIVIST ACTION PLANS AT THE MICRO, MESO, AND MACRO LEVELS

"Action is an integral and indispensable component of transformative learning" (Mezirow, 1991, p. 209). A transformative andragogy teaches future leaders to be proactive versus reactive, to embrace conflict rather than avoid it, and to engage in what Fine, Weiss, and Powell (1997) called opportunities for "creative analysis of difference, power and privilege" (p. 249).

Reminded that there are always consequences to our ideas, words, and actions, Bogotch (2002) found that whenever educators act on their passionate beliefs, it can and does make a difference. The possibility for social change by educational activists is anchored in an acceptance that "the relations between knowledge, power, and social change continually need to be interrogated" (Popkewitz, 1999, p. 8).

Through the social-action approach (see Banks, 1997), adult learners are encouraged to make decisions on important social issues and to take actions to help solve them. Activists' action plans at the micro, meso, and macro levels help future leaders for social justice, equity, and excellence move beyond guilt for failure toward responsibility for success. By assessing and examining current procedures and then reordering and restructuring their practice according to a new agenda of social action, adult learners engage in a developmental process of "deconstruction and reconstruction."

Adult learners discuss what they might do at the school level, district/community level, and state level to implement policies and practices that are truly just, equitable, and inclusive of all members of the school community. Recognizing that differences do matter, students are encouraged to keep in mind that all major documents, work systems, and processes should be based upon equity, fairness, and justice.

Through activist action plans, future leaders first identify issues that can trigger conflicts (i.e., unequal distribution of material/social resources or differing values, beliefs, and cultural expressions), and then they develop practical, doable strategies for avoiding them and/or resolving them. Adult learners also address the issue of action versus inaction. Through a deeper sense of awareness and acknowledgment, students are instructed to name possible acts of commission, as well as more subtle acts of omission. The ramifications of such decisions are examined, discussed, and thoroughly dissected in light of course content, new understandings, and personal growth.

According to Cranton (1992), action is the litmus test of transformative learning, it is evidence of changed perspectives. By increasing their tactical awareness and acknowledgment of what "is" and what "ought to be," many future leaders in this study reportedly began to build a personal confidence and a professional desire to work for collective change. While they didn't necessarily become active defenders for social justice in schools, they did indicate the importance of action for social justice and began to entertain ways they could actually act upon their newly found set of beliefs and notions.

Analysis of the data revealed a perceived increase in their willingness to engage in and facilitate critical, constructive inquiry regarding issues of social justice and equity. As students grow in a realization of their own agency, the goal of critical social theory is for them to increase their commitment and ability to validate the cultural, intellectual, and emotional identities of people from underrepresented groups through policy praxis.

"How will I make the changes happen that I know need to occur?" "Do my ideas represent the school's populations, even those who are not in the majority?" "Will all the silenced voices be heard? How in the world will I advocate for everyone that needs it? Will I remember and apply what I've learned? Will I be bold enough?" "How do I totally erase the guilt and move forward?" Questions such as these sprinkled the pages of the future leaders' journals. In moving from self-reported increased awareness and acknowledgment to self-reported increased action, they reflected on their ability to be change agents and even questioned the goals of their preparation program.

> I know these presentations are very beneficial to my understanding of becoming "a needed change agent" but they surely cause me a lot of stress! Presenting these groups in isolation gives me a broader perspective on the same injustices going on today that have traveled through history with certain groups.
>
> To a certain degree, the information that I heard was painful. History is becoming more and more insufferable. My ancestors did this damage to these people. The effect is still being felt today. I have a responsibility to help correct the situation. I need to research, read, dig for information in all aspects of other races to help understand how I will be able to make the greatest impact as an administrator.
>
> I was astonished at the terrified feelings one of the panel members shared about riding the bus with American children of different cultural backgrounds than herself. This helped me to realize that as an administrator it is important that I make all children and staff feel safe at school and comfortable so their learning environment can be as productive as possible.

After reading Delpit and Spring I think it would make a fantastic discussion to look at the goals of the Ed Leadership program . . . it has some pretty lofty, revolutionary, social justice goals. Are these goals more pipe dreams, while American culture continues to put more and more power and wealth in fewer and fewer (mostly white) hands? Or does the department really feel it is sending change agents out to lead the public schools of this area?

These changes in which I view the world must be a catalyst for action. It is working too. This becomes evident each day when I promote new conversations, when I find myself offering new arguments in the presence of racist comments, and when I envision my multi-cultural role as an educational administrator.

During their comprehensive, yearlong, full-time structured internship, some of the future leaders were able to put their action plans into practice. Their implementation efforts yielded mixed results in terms of behaviors, boundaries, alternatives, and consequences. The adult learners struggled with their role as student intern, with their ability to be proactive versus reactive, and with their willingness to embrace conflict rather than avoid it.

Here are just a few samples, of many, illustrating future leaders' desire and capability to take action when needed. The first reflection, "Donuts with Dad," represents an intern's conviction and creative ability to include *all*. The second entry, "ESL Policy," portrays an intern's frustration and resolve to meet the needs of *all*, The third story, "Late Bus Duty," illustrates an intern's uncertainty in working with others for the benefit of *all*.

[Donuts with Dad] Every year the PTA hosts "Donuts with Dad." This is a two-day event that takes place in the mornings in the school cafeteria. One of my normal daily duties is to escort my bus load of low income children (who have a 40 minute bus ride) to their free and reduced breakfast. This bunch of children is for the most part well behaved at school, they do their best, and they have supportive parents. However, many are from single parent families, they have limited financial resources, they lack private transportation, and they often face big challenges in their day-to-day family life. Well, on Thursday, half of the school students had "Donuts with Dad." I had to march my bus children in through the festivities to pick up their breakfast and then they were relocated outside to the picnic tables to eat. This troubled me tremendously. To be displaced out of the cafeteria so that everyone else can come and have a special breakfast with Dad was a mean and insensitive thing to do. Let me provide a mental image. Picture me leading a group of about 45 to 60 predominately African American children through a cafeteria full of predominately white children and their relatives and then having to sit outside at a picnic table so that those attending the breakfast would not be disturbed or crowded. I refused to parade those kids through their own cafeteria again like a herd of passing animals. With some help, and some kind folks, we changed the scene for Friday morning. I recruited all four of the available male faculty to act as stand-in relatives.

I also recruited the male mentors already working with some of our students and I called the local churches to ask for a few volunteers. In addition, I talked with the PTA president and she assured me that there were enough donuts for every child in the school and that my bus kids were more than welcome to come. So Friday, when the bus arrived, I told the children that we had several community guests and some teachers who wanted donuts but had no one to eat with and asked if they would be willing to escort some guests. Needless to say, the children were more than happy to oblige!

[ESL Policy] I feel sorry for the students and staff who are involved with this program and how the district has let them down. It is no secret that the building sites were not given adequate support or resources for this program to work. Most of the time we feel overwhelmed, exhausted and would much rather give up and complain rather than do something about it. I need to let go of that attitude and remain committed to being an instructional leader for ALL students. With that being said, I have chosen to do some things to enhance the program and create more resources and awareness. I recruited undergrad teacher ed. volunteers to work with individual students in the ESL program and I have organized and planned monthly ESL workshops geared to helping the regular classroom teachers deal with ESL students.

[Late Bus Duty] One of the duties that I have chosen for myself is being in the gym on a daily basis waiting for the late busses to arrive (3:55 pm–4:20 pm). It is a duty I truly enjoy as I have found many opportunities to get to know students and staff on a more personal level. There are some staff members who chose this as the duty they preferred to be given and others who are clearly fulfilling an assigned responsibility only (two-week rotation). Most of the children waiting for the late busses are minority students who live on the other side of town. They are waiting for the busses to return from the first run of dropping off the local, neighborhood kids. Gazing across the gym, one of the teachers on duty remarked to me, "Well this is a completely different culture from the rest of the school, don't you think?" I was not sure what she was getting at so I suggested that it certainly was unique to see students of all different grade levels together in the gym. The teacher informed me that that was not what she meant. She said, "Look at all these troublemakers in the same room. This doesn't happen in any other area of the school." The conversation continued with the teacher telling me that cluster grouping (placing similarly situated minority students together in classrooms) was a bad idea and that she couldn't believe the administration had decided to try that this year. I let the teacher know that these were wonderful children, not troublemakers, and that we clearly had different ideas on the topic. This exchange lasted no longer than three minutes but I have been unable to get it out of my mind. With the district-wide goal of increasing minority student achievement and the emphasis on equity training for staff, I am completely dumbfounded by her remarks. My role as an intern places me in a difficult position in terms of how I can respond to these situations. But, as a future school leader, it is imperative that courageous conversations about race take place. In thinking about this situation, and others I have encountered thus far, I have many questions . . . these questions haunt my thoughts as I struggle to make sense of how a leader changes the mindset of the people he/she works with on both a personal and professional level. There are no easy answers here, at least I know that much!

SOCIAL AGENCY SITE VISITS

Another suggested experiential opportunity for future leaders is to visit local social service agencies. Together with three or four others in the class who chose the same social context issue to study in depth, adult learners conduct the class on a scheduled day. They were expected to find, assign, and distribute additional, pertinent readings (e.g., personal narratives) in presenting the social issue and its impact on the educational, schooling, and advancement of children across the United States.

For the history, they are to present no more than three to five important historical events and three to five major educational policies to help others understand how that social context issue has evolved and how history lives on and affects the present (e.g., philosophically, economically, politically, socially, and culturally). Presentations include:

(1) demographic information (national, state, and local figures),
(2) values considered representative of the majority of people affected by this social issue,
(3) discussion of their schooling experiences,
(4) stereotypes associated with people in that group, and
(5) implications for school leaders in addressing this social context issue and working with students, parents, and families affected by this issue.

Possible social context issues, organizations, agencies, and advocates include the following: adolescents, health issues, mental health, family resources, housing, crisis, violence, learning disabilities, teenage pregnancy, homelessness, English language learners (ELLs), physical/mental/domestic abuse, poverty, drug/alcohol abuse, volunteers, counseling, child custody, criminal justice, gangs, gays/lesbians, immigrants, at-risk, churches, prisons, communities in schools, school psychologists, social workers, self-regulatory organizations (SROs), community resource centers, rehabs, group homes, McKinney-Vento coordinators, Division of Child Protection and Permanency (DYFS), Long-acting reversible contraception (LARC), and so forth.

Most importantly, future leaders are instructed to present three to five examples of culturally relevant/responsive instructional strategies that have been proven successful in working with students and parents affected by this

social context issue. They are asked to highlight successful schools, programs, and teaching methods that improve literacy skills and increase student
achievement and to discuss best practices and practical strategies/approaches
for working with teachers (who may be prejudiced and feel overworked,
underpaid, pressured, and frustrated) to create academically successful
schools that are socially just and equitable.

Adult learners are instructed to use any format they want for the site visit
project, although they are encouraged to keep lecturing to a minimum, and to
actively involve class members as much as possible, particularly sharing of
responses to the material presented. Here are a few of their reflections:

> This was one of the most beneficial aspects of the course. I loved the collabora-
> tion and information gathering and sharing that took place in preparation for this
> component of the class.
>
> Wow. I must admit that, at first, I wasn't too excited about traveling all over
> the place to these different locations. Now that we've visited folks on their
> own ground and in their own space, I clearly see the benefit of these visits. We
> would not have learned and experienced what we did if we had just stayed in
> the proverbial Ivory Tower.
>
> Actually going to and spending time at the student Learning Center in the heart
> of the projects was the most memorable experience for me this semester. I had no
> idea that such places existed. I was so inspired by the dedication and determina-
> tion of the director and the teachers. These adults really care about these kids and
> the kids are so eager to share what they've learned. They seemed happy, safe,
> and proud. I'm seriously considering tutoring there once a week now. Thanks.
>
> Our visit to the Community Outreach Center was eye-opening for me. I didn't
> realize that such resources are out there or that so many people took advantage
> of such services. As a future administrator, I am grateful to know about this
> place. I got the contact info for the psychologists, the social workers, and the
> community liaison lady and will call them when needed.

SCHOOL/DISTRICT EQUITY AUDITS

As adult learners consider possible actions and realistic approaches, they are
encouraged to consider in depth the possible outcomes of the strategy, the
risks and obstacles involved, the timeline for implementation, the supports
needed, and where they might find them. One specific technique recommended for all future leaders and their schools and school districts is the use
of educational equity audits (see Skrla, Garcia, Scheurich, & Nolly, 2002).

With historical roots connected to the civil rights movement, the curriculum auditing movement (see English, 1988), and the state accountability
movement, educational equity profiles systematically examine school dimensions such as teacher quality equity, programmatic equity, and achievement

equity. By doing this, leaders for social justice become empowered with school and community members to envision, define, and work equity, toward a more humane society that removes all forms of injustice.

Equity audits are a leadership tool that can be used to guide schools in working toward social justice, equity, and excellence. Equity audits use district, school, and classroom data to identify (uncover), address (understand), and remove (change) systemic patterns of inequality that come from inside the school.

Using data that their school and district already collect to identify systemic patterns of inequity internal to the school, patterns that prevent, or form barriers to, our being equally successful with all student groups, future leaders are encouraged to identify patterns in school personnel, as well as students. They are instructed to differentiate students by race, class, gender, first language, and sexual orientation. Possible areas of inequity included:

(1) student achievement (learning, growth, grades, test scores, classes, teachers, type of diploma, career choices/options),
(2) teacher quality (advanced degrees, years of experience, certifications, stability),
(3) educational programs (representation in gifted and talented programs, advanced placement courses, college track courses, special education, student organizations, foreign language programs, career/technology/ vocational education programs),
(4) student discipline (student/teacher referrals, suspensions, In school suspension (ISS) and Out of school suspension (OSS), types of violations, types of consequences),
(5) student attendance (retention rates, dropout rates, truancy policies), and
(6) participation in extracurricular activities (academic, athletic, community, transportation, costs, notifications).

The purpose of this activity is to develop an Action Plan for implementing change that will assist future leaders in creating both an equitable and excellent school. Given the results of their Demographic Data Questionnaire (DDQ) (see Frattura & Capper, 2007), adult learners list the top three inequities that exist in their school/district. They are asked to hypothesize why these inequities are occurring and to make note of the issues that are not the focus of school or district data collection.

Next, based on their DDQ data, analyses, and hypotheses, as well as course readings and discussions, future leaders are asked to identify three changes/ recommendations that they feel need to be made to their school/district in order to remedy these inequities. They are reminded to prioritize their list of changes and to consider the "doability" of the change they would like to see in their school. They list the audiences/targets/facilitators who have the power and commitment to do something with their findings, and find the appropriate way to deliver them.

Finally, future leaders select one change they feel needs to be made in their school/district in order for their school to be both equitable and excellent and develop an action plan to make that change happen. They outline the specific steps they will need to take in order to implement their idea for change. (They consider these steps a road map—observable, measurable behaviors they will take in order to make this change happen.)

Adult learners are encouraged to consider both short-term and long-term actions (they think three, six, and nine months down the road) and to consider how their actions respond to the specific inequity both reactively and proactively. They also need to consider timelines, involvement of personnel, resources, and an evaluation method by which they will measure their progress.

CONCLUSION

Social justice is both a process and a goal. According to Bell (1997), "social justice includes a vision of society in which the distribution of resources is equitable and all members are physically and psychologically safe and secure" (p. 3). Ayers, Hunt, and Quinn (1998) added that teaching for social justice "arouses students, engages them in a quest to identify obstacles to their full humanity, to their freedom" (p. xvii), and ends in action to move against those obstacles. Preparing transformative leaders to accept this challenge necessitates both a close examination of personal beliefs coupled with a critical analysis of professional behavior.

Together, these processes can lead to a transformation of one's own agency, as well as a sense of social responsibility toward and with others. The alternative andragogy described in this book is aimed at developing such leaders for social justice, equity, and excellence. By weaving theory into practice, future leaders can grow in their awareness, acknowledgment, and action toward a more humane society that removes all forms of injustice.

CRITICAL QUESTIONS

1. *Identify a current school, district, or state policy that addresses the needs of some students while simultaneously neglecting the needs of other students. When was the policy implemented and by whom? Can the policy be redesigned to better meet the needs of all students? Why/why not? How? How can school leaders realistically influence the direction of education in this nation?*

2. *What social service agencies in your community are geared toward help-ing school-age children and their families? What partnerships have been formed between them and the schools? Why/why not? How? What part-nerships might be formed?*
3. *What student achievement data is currently reported on your school, dis-trict, and statewide website? What data isn't reported? Why?*

REFERENCES

Astin, A. W. (1993). *What matters in college? Four critical years revisited.* San Fran-cisco, CA: Jossey-Bass.

Ayers, W., Hunt, J. A., & Quinn, T. (Eds.). (1998). *Teaching for social justice. A democracy and education reader.* New York, NY: New Press, Teachers College.

Banks, J. (1997). *Educating citizens in a multicultural society.* New York, NY: Teach-ers College.

Bell, L. A. (1997). Theoretical foundations for social justice education. In M. Adams, L. A. Bell, & P. Griffin (Eds.), *Teaching for diversity and social justice* (pp. 3–15). New York, NY: Routledge.

Bogotch, I. (2002). Educational leadership and social justice: Practice into theory. *Journal of School Leadership, 12*(2), 138–156.

Cochran-Smith, M. (1998). Teaching for social change: Toward a grounded theory of teacher education. In A. Hargreaves, A. Lieberman, M. Fullan, & D. Hopkins (Eds.), *The international handbook of educational change* (pp. 916–951). Dor-drecht, The Netherlands: Kluwer Academic.

Cranton, P. (1992). *Working with adult learners.* Toronto, Canada: Wall & Emerson.

Dunn, J. M. (1987). Personal beliefs and public policy. In F. S. Bolin & J. M. Falk (Eds.), *Teacher renewal: Professional issues, personal choices* (pp. 76–86). New York, NY: Teachers College.

English, F. (1988). *Curriculum auditing.* Lancaster, PA: Technomic.

Fine, M., Weiss, L., & Powell, L. (1997). Communities of difference: A critical look at desegregated spaces created for and by youth. *Harvard Educational Review, 67*(2), 247–284.

Frattura, E., & Capper, C. (2007). *Leading for social justice: Transforming schools for all learners.* Thousand Oaks, CA: Corwin.

Freire, P. (1970). *Pedagogy of the oppressed.* New York, NY: Seabury.

Freire, P., & Macedo, D. (1995). A dialogue: Culture, language, and race. *Harvard Educational Review, 65*(3), 377–402.

Lindsey, R., Robins, K., & Terrell, R. (1999). *Cultural proficiency: A manual for school leaders.* Thousand Oaks, CA: Corwin.

Mezirow, J. (1990). *Fostering critical reflection in adulthood: A guide to transforma-tive and emancipatory learning.* San Francisco, CA: Jossey-Bass.

Mezirow, J. (1991). *Transformative dimensions of adult learning.* San Francisco, CA: Jossey-Bass.

Oakes, J., & Lipton, M. (1999). *Teaching to change the world*. Boston, MA: McGraw-Hill College.

Popkewitz, T. (1999). Introduction: Critical traditions, modernisms, and the "posts." In T.S. Popkewitz & L. Fender (Eds.), *Critical theories in education: Changing terrains of knowledge and politics* (pp. 1–13). New York, NY: Routledge.

Rapp, D., Silent X, & Silent Y. (2001). The implications of raising one's voice in educational leadership doctoral programs: Women's stories of fear, retaliation, and silence. *Journal of School Leadership, 11*(4), 279–295.

Scott, W., & Hart, D. (1979). *Organizational America: Can individual freedom survive the security it promises?* Boston, MA: Houghton Mifflin.

Sirontnik, K., & Kimball, K. (1996). Preparing educators for leadership: In praise of experience. *Journal of School Leadership, 6*(2), 180–201.

Skrla, L., Garcia, J., Scheurich, J., & Nolly, G. (2002, August). *Educational equity profiles: Practical leadership tools for equitable and excellent schools*. Paper presented at the convention of the National Council of Professors of Educational Administration, Burlington, VT.

Trueba, H. T. (1999). *Latinos unidos: From cultural diversity to politics of solidarity*. Lanham, MD: Rowman & Littlefield.

Chapter 7

Recent Research for Section II

INTRODUCTION

Throughout the three chapters in "Section II: Transformative Andragogical Practice and the Centrality of Experience," the three theoretical perspectives of adult learning theory, transformative learning theory, and critical social theory are interwoven with the three andragogical strategies of critical reflection, rational discourse, and policy praxis to increase future and current leaders' awareness, acknowledgment, and action for social justice, equity, and excellence.

Employing a critical, transformative andragogy requires professors and principals to be active facilitators and co-learners who go beyond just meeting the expressed needs of the learner or the teacher. Through a wide array of roles, methods, and techniques, they need to take on the responsibility for growth by questioning the learner's expectations and beliefs. Transformative learning is a process of critical self-reflection that can be stimulated by people, events, or changes in context that challenge the learner's basic assumptions about the world.

This chapter, written for the second edition of this book, reviews the literature on the topics discussed in section II. This literature was published during the years following the publication of the first edition. The first section deals with critical reflection, discussing reasons for the difficulties of educators who seek to engage their students in meaningful critical reflection. The second section covers the literature about rational discourse. Both critical reflection and rational discourse are key elements in transformative learning.

CRITICAL REFLECTION

The concepts of *reflection* and *reflective practice* have become key components of teachers' training and professional development (Clark, Brown, &
Jandildinov, 2016; Segall & Gaudelli, 2007). Reflection helps teachers
reconstruct experiences and make sense out of them (Blumberg, 2015).
While reflecting, they reorganize their comprehension and feelings, leading
to deeper insights as a result of self-knowledge (Stevens & Cooper, 2009).
A high level of reflection can transform their understanding as it may help
them to overcome their misrepresentations and thus become more efficient
(Raelin, 2010).

Critical reflection is the central process in teachers' transformative learning, leading to some fundamental changes in perspective (Hanson, 2013). In
the social justice context, critical reflection allows teachers to understand and
investigate dominant social norms, systemic influences, and basic assumptions and values that have unconsciously created their professional identity
and practice. If there is no regular critique, these norms and assumptions may
continue constituting barriers to inclusion and access for some young people,
especially those from minority groups.

Through critical reflection on one's own practice, an understanding can
develop of how one's interpersonal interactions influence others, both positively and negatively (Morgan, 2017). This type of critical reflection facili-
tates the development of "emotional insight . . . alongside critical awareness,
self-knowledge and deepening understanding of the other" (West, 2010,
p. 66). Moreover, critical reflection is perceived as a tool challenging the
dynamics of traditional hierarchical power in teaching and learning relationships between adults and young people (Nabavi & Lund, 2010). When
dynamics of power are understood and challenged appropriately, democratic
learning communities can more fully realize their potential.

However, recent research has revealed that many teacher educators, as
well as other professional educators, find it difficult to consistently engage
their students in a higher-level critical reflection both in classrooms (Coulson & Harvey, 2013; Ryan & Townsend, 2012) and in clinical field place-
ments (Dyke, Harding, & Liddon, 2008; Jacobs, 2006). Some learners who
are asked to reflect critically on their practices engage in technical-rational
reflections, failing to refer to their emotions (Karban & Smith, 2009). Not all
educators succeed in engaging students in critical reflection of the sort that
leads to transformation, because learners may question things without changing them (Cranton, 2006).

Some researchers attribute the difficulty of educators who seek to engage
their students in meaningful critical reflection to a lack of consensus on its
actual definition (Smith, 2011). Various scholars have attributed different

meanings to the practice of reflection (D'Cruz, Gillingham, & Melendez, 2006; Ruch, 2009; White, Fook, & Gardner, 2006). One of the significant differences between such scholars stems from their different ways of understanding the word "critical" (Theobald, Gardner, & Long, 2017), which may be used in the sense of analytical, that is, pertaining to the capacity to think in a conceptual and methodical manner; though it may also be used to connote judgment, as meant when speaking of being criticized.

This results in some scholars' preference to avoid the word "critical" altogether. Stedmon and Sallos (2009), for example, point to the danger of critical reflection being perceived as "surveillance" or "inquisition" (p. 4). Similarly, Oterholm (2009) felt that the word "critical" had too many possible negative meanings in Norwegian translation and decided to use "challenging" rather than "critical." On the other hand, from a more analytical point of view, Crawford (2012) suggests that "critical" means being "open, honest and thoughtful", and that reflection becomes more effective when it also takes into account knowledge based on research and literature (p. 171).

Another explanation for the difficulty to engage students in effective critical reflection may be the lack of effective approaches to facilitating critical reflection in courses (Ajayi, 2011). Goldstein (2007) described herself as an educator who had "grasped what we, as critical educators, were supposed to do, but was unable to put the theory into practice . . . I could practice 'critical theory' but not 'critical pedagogy'" (p. 17). She warned against a contradictory situation where educators internalize the theory, but fail to "interrogate the ways in which they too are complicit in the dominant culture forms and practices that continue to marginalize their students" (p. 19).

Moreover, when the emphasis is placed on reporting outcomes and lessons learned rather than on the complexities of the process, the term "critical reflection" may result in "conceptual slipperiness" (Chiu, 2006). Development has transformative potential only when participation and critical reflection are affirmed as central to the process (Chambers, 2005).

RATIONAL DISCOURSE

Rational discourse was found to be a central component of transformative learning (Lavrysh, 2015). It is a catalyst for transformation, as it leads the various learners to explore and express the depth and meaning of their worldviews (Fook & Sidhu, 2013), "working out" their transformation by coming in touch with their beliefs, then explaining and challenging them. After completing a process of rational discourse, which allows participants to become aware of a shift in their personal perspectives, their ability to visualize and discuss their possibilities for new roles, relationships, and actions expands considerably (Brown & Brown, 2015).

Taylor and Cranton (2012) placed three main themes at the core of the transformative learning process: experience, critical reflection, and rational discourse. The transformative process begins with actual experience; however, the experience does not suffice to trigger the process. Experience can become transformative only when it goes hand in hand with critical reflection, with the adult learner questioning assumptions and beliefs that he or she has used to interpret the meaning of past experiences.

Experience and critical reflection are then activated through rational discourse, which is the decisive factor in promoting transformation (Baumgartner, 2012). Dialogue can foster connections with others in similar circumstances through storytelling and reflective sense-making. Talking with others on a one-to-one basis, in small groups or in educational settings, initiates a "better understanding of self through engagement with others" (Taylor & Cranton, 2012, p. 8), which may ultimately lead to a transformed perspective (Taylor & Hill, 2016).

According to Mezirow (2007), "The assumptions of rational discourse are that beliefs should contain no logical contradictions, reasons for believing them can be advanced and assessed, concepts will become more intelligible when analyzed and we have criteria with which to know when the belief is justified or not." Moreover, he argues that the ideal conditions for rational discourse are the same as for effective adult learning.

Therefore, participants must have a sense of trust and empathic solidarity with their interlocutors; accurate and complete information; freedom from coercion and distorting self-deception; and equal opportunity to participate in the discussion, to have their voices heard and understood. Participants in an ideal adult discourse will also have previously learned to consider evidence and evaluate arguments objectively; respect alternative perspectives; reflect critically upon assumptions and their consequences; and accept an informed, objective, rational consensus as a legitimate test of validity of a certain belief until further evidence or arguments are received.

In the context of social justice, Mezirow (2007) went on to claim that freedom, equality, participatory democracy, tolerance, solidarity, caring, and inclusion are social values that are integrated into the ideal process of making sense through collaborative discourse. Obviously, like any other ideal concept, ideal discourse seldom exists in actual experience. We can all point to the destructive distortions caused by inequality in the distribution of power and resources related to race or ethnic origin, gender, and class. However, as an ideal construct, this model of undistorted communication provides us with a goal and standard by which to judge our efforts both as learners and as educators.

CONCLUSION

Transformative learning may occur as a result of a life crisis or may be precipitated by challenging interactions with others, by participation in carefully designed exercises and activities, or by stimulation through reading or other experiences. The three chapters in section II demonstrate how by being actively engaged in a number of assignments requiring the examination of ontological and epistemological assumptions, values and beliefs, context and experience, and competing worldviews, adult learners (principals and teachers) can be better equipped to guide and work with others in translating their perspectives, perceptions, and goals into agendas for social change.

The exploration of new understandings and the synthesis of new information, followed by their integration through personal and professional processes, can lead current and future educational leaders and their school faculties to a broader, more inclusive approach in addressing issues of student learning and equity in their schools and districts.

KEY IDEAS IN THIS CHAPTER

1. *Critical reflection is a key process in educators' transformative learning, leading to fundamental changes in perspective. In the social justice context, critical reflection makes it possible to examine dominant social norms, systemic influences, and basic assumptions and values that unconsciously affect professional identity and practice. However, researchers have found that it is quite difficult to consistently engage educators in a higher-level critical reflection.*
2. *Another key process in educators' transformative learning is rational discourse. Leading educators to express and investigate the deep meaning of their beliefs, rational discourse contributes to change by contacting educators' worldviews and then explaining and challenging them. In the context of social justice, values such as equality, participatory democracy, tolerance, solidarity, caring, and inclusion are integrated into the ideal process of making sense through collaborative discourse.*

REFERENCES

Ajayi, L. (2011). Teaching alternative licensed literacy teachers to learn from practice: A critical reflection model. *Teacher Education Quarterly*, *38*(3), 169–189.
Baumgartner, L. M. (2012). Mezirow's theory of transformative learning from 1975 to present. In E. W. Taylor & P. Cranton (Eds.), *The handbook of transformative*

learning: Theory, research, and practice (pp. 99–115). San Francisco, CA: Jossey-Bass.

Blumberg, P. (2015). How critical reflection benefits faculty as they implement learner-centered teaching. *New Directions for Teaching and Learning, 144*, 87–97.

Brown, P. P., & Brown, C. S. (2015). Transformative learning theory in gerontology: Nontraditional students. *Educational Gerontology, 41*(2), 136–148.

Chambers, R. (2005). *Ideas for development*. London, UK: Earthscan.

Chiu, L. F. (2006). Critical reflection: More than nuts and bolts. *Action Research, 4*(2), 182–203.

Clark, J. S., Brown, J. S., & Jandildinov, M. (2016). Enriching preservice teachers' critical reflection through an international videoconference discussion. *Technology, Pedagogy and Education, 25*(4), 431–450.

Coulson, D., & Harvey, M. (2013). Scaffolding student reflection for experience-based learning: A framework. *Teaching in Higher Education, 18*(4), 401–413.

Cranton, P. (2006). *Understanding and promoting transformative learning: A guide for educators of adults* (2nd ed.). San Francisco, CA: Jossey-Bass.

Crawford, K. (2012). *Interprofessional collaboration in social work practice*. London, UK: Sage.

D'Cruz, H., Gillingham, P., & Melendez, S. (2006). Reflexivity, its meanings and relevance for social work: A critical review of the literature. *British Journal of Social Work, 37*(1), 73–90.

Dyke, M., Harding, A., & Liddon, S. (2008). How can online observation support the assessment and feedback, on classroom performance, to trainee teachers at a distance and in real time? *Journal of Further and Higher Education, 32*(1), 37–46.

Fook, C. Y., & Sidhu, G. K. (2013). Promoting transformative learning through formative assessment in higher education. *ASEAN Journal of Teaching & Learning in Higher Education, 5*(1), 1–11.

Goldstein, R. A. (2007). The perilous pitfalls of praxis: Critical pedagogy as "regime of truth." In R. A. Goldstein (Ed.), *Useful theory: Making critical education practical* (pp. 15–30). New York, NY: Peter Lang.

Hanson, C. (2013). Exploring dimensions of critical reflection in activist-facilitator practice. *Journal of Transformative Education, 11*(1), 70 89.

Jacobs, J. (2006). Supervision for social justice: Supporting critical reflection. *Teacher Education Quarterly, 33*(4), 23–39.

Karban, K., & Smith, S. (2009). Developing critical reflection within an interprofessional learning programme. In H. Bradbury, N. Frost, S. Kilminster, & M. Zukas (Eds.), *Beyond reflective practice* (pp. 170–181). London, UK: Routledge.

Lavrysh, Y. (2015). Transformative learning as a factor of lifelong learning by the example of vocational education in Canada. *Comparative Professional Pedagogy, 5*(4), 62–67.

Mezirow, J. (2007). Adult education and empowerment for individual and community development. In B. Connolly, T. Fleming, D. McCormack, & A. Ryan, *Radical learning for liberation 2* (pp. 19–23). Dublin, Ireland: Maynooth Adult and Community Education.

Morgan, A. (2017). Cultivating critical reflection: Educators making sense and meaning of professional identity and relational dynamics in complex practice. *Teaching Education, 28*(1), 41–55.

Nabavi, M., & Lund, D. (2010). Youth and social justice: A conversation on collaborative activism. In W. Linds, L. Goulet, & A. Sammel (Eds.), *Emancipatory practices: Adult/youth engagement for social and environmental justice* (pp. 3–14). Rotterdam, The Netherlands: Sense.

Oterholm, I. (2009). Online critical reflection in social work education. *European Journal of Social Work, 12*(3), 363–375.

Raelin, J. A. (2010). Work-based learning: Valuing practice as an educational event. In D. M. Qualters (Ed.), *Experiential education: Making the most of learning outside the classroom* (pp. 39–46). San Francisco, CA: Jossey-Bass.

Ruch, G. (2009). Identifying "the critical" in a relationship-based model of reflection. *European Journal of Social Work, 12*(3), 349–362.

Ryan, P. A., & Townsend, J. S. (2012). Promoting critical reflection in teacher education through popular media. *Action in Teacher Education, 34*(3), 239–248.

Segall, A., & Gaudelli, W. (2007). Reflecting socially on social issues in a social studies methods course. *Teaching Education, 18*(1), 77–92.

Smith, E. (2011). Teaching critical reflection. *Teaching in Higher Education, 16*(2), 211–223.

Stedmon, S. J., & Sallos, R. (Eds.). (2009). *Reflective practice in psychotheraphy and counselling.* Maidenhead, UK: Open University.

Stevens, D. D., & Cooper, J. E. (2009). *Journal keeping: How to use reflective writing for learning, teaching, professional insight and positive change.* Sterling, VA: Stylus.

Taylor, E. W., & Cranton, P. (2012). Transformative learning theory: Seeking a more unified theory. In E. W. Taylor & P. Cranton (Eds.), *The handbook of transformative learning: Theory, research, and practice* (pp. 3–20). San Francisco, CA: Jossey-Bass.

Taylor, M. B., & Hill, L. H. (2016). Employing transformative learning theory in the design and implementation of a curriculum for court-ordered participants in a parent education class. *Journal of Transformative Education, 14*(3), 254–271.

Theobald, J., Gardner, F., & Long, N. (2017). Teaching critical reflection in social work field education. *Journal of Social Work Education, 53*(2), 300–311.

West, L. (2010). Really reflexive practice: Auto/biographical research and struggles for a critical reflexivity. In H. Bradbury, N. Frost, S. Kilminster, & M. Zukas (Eds.), *Beyond reflective practice: New approaches to professional lifelong learning* (pp. 66–80). London, UK: Routledge.

White, S., Fook, J., & Gardner. F. (Eds.). (2006). *Critical reflection in health and social care.* London, UK: Open University.

Chapter 8

Concluding Discussion

In the forward of Capper's *Educational Administration in a Pluralistic Society*, Sleeter (1993) draws on Giroux's (1983) description of the type of administrator she would like to see advocating for equality and social justice in schools: "These are transformative intellectuals who are both active, reflective scholars and practitioners," who "engage in political interests that are emancipatory in nature" (p. ix). The andragogical strategies described in this book can help future leaders for social justice, equity, and excellence develop such skills.

By being actively engaged in a number of assignments requiring the examination of ontological and epistemological assumptions, values and beliefs, context and experience, and competing worldviews, adult learners will be better equipped to work with and guide others in translating their perspectives, perceptions, and goals into agendas for social change. The exploration of new understandings, the synthesis of new information, and the integration of these insights throughout personal and professional spheres can lead future educational leaders to a broader, more inclusive approach in addressing equity issues. When discussing educators' agency for transformation, Freire (1998) aptly explained, "It is true that education is not the ultimate lever for social transformation, but without it transformation cannot occur" (p. 37).

Through a wide array of roles, methods, and techniques, preparation programs must encourage adult learners to question their expectations, beliefs, and actions. Through critical reflection, rational discourse, and policy praxis, preparation programs must implement ways for future leaders for social justice and equity to grow in awareness, acknowledgment, and action!

According to Giroux (1992), "if students are going to learn how to take risks, to develop healthy skepticism towards all master narratives, to recognize the power relations that offer them the opportunity to speak in particular ways, and be willing to critically confront their role as critical citizens who can animate a democratic culture, they need to see such behavior demonstrated in the social practices and subject positions that teachers live out and not merely propose" (p. 141).

Given the relevance of beliefs and the difficulty in changing them, this book can help educational administration programs begin to better understand the connections between leadership preparation experiences and the knowledge, dispositions, and skills garnered. Leadership for social justice requires a close examination of personal beliefs coupled with a critical analysis of professional behavior.

While convincing research suggests that beliefs are the best predictors of individual behavior and that educators' beliefs influence their perceptions, judgments, and practices, research also states that beliefs are hard and highly resistant to change (Bandura, 1986; Dewey, 1938; Pajares, 1992; Rokeach, 1968). Understanding the nature of beliefs, attitudes, and values is essential to understanding leaders' choices, decisions, and effectiveness regarding issues of diversity, social justice, and equity. Assessing beliefs in an effort to make them known and subject to critical analysis is an important initial step in the process.

The key to change is new experience. According to Kotter and Cohen (2002), "people rarely change through a rational process of analyze-think-change" (p. 11). They are much more likely to change in a see-feel-change sequence. This point is particularly noteworthy for the preparation of leaders for social justice, equity, and excellence. It suggests that greater exposure to and involvement in transformative learning opportunities might lead future leaders to greater understanding and acceptance of diverse groups, greater openness to different ways of thinking, greater awareness of social inequities, and, hopefully greater social activism.

Assuming that administrators with positive attitudes and increased intellectual flexibility, tolerance, and respect are more prone to behave appropriately and constructively in educational situations involving students of diverse backgrounds, it makes sense for preparation programs to restructure their teaching to include transformative learning strategies. This assumption is supported by Larke (1990), who stated "studies show a high correlation exists among educators' sensitivity (attitudes, beliefs and behaviors toward students of other cultures), knowledge, and application of cultural awareness information and minority students' successful academic performance" (p. 24).

According to Scheurich and Skrla (2003), "The success of our society will soon be directly dependent on our ability as educators to be successful with children of color, with whom we have not been very successful in the past" (p. 5). These alarming gaps challenge us to dig deeper inside the schools for more subtle causes. Scott (2001) calls these internal causes of inequity *systemic inequities* because they are built systematically into the processes and procedures of the system that is the school. A school culture that perpetuates the status quo and turns a blind eye to the social injustices that permeate our schools is not really "excellent." As such, excellence and equity must be pursued concurrently to assure that all students are served well and that all are encouraged to perform at their highest level.

Equity audits are a practical, easy-to-apply tool that leaders for social justice can use to objectively identify educational inequalities. By studying schools that teach similar populations of students from similar geographical regions, it is impossible to ignore the role that schools play in the achievement of all students. Data is powerful; it separates personal agendas from organizational necessities. By collecting, analyzing, and then exhibiting data in a transparent way, leaders for social justice, equity, and excellence can illuminate certain disparities in practices, certain deficiencies in systems, and certain gaps in outcomes.

"The fact that, broadly speaking, our children experience differential levels of success in school that is distributed along race and social class lines continues to be the overridingly central problem of education" (Skrla, Scheurich, Johnson, & Koschoreck, 2001, p. 239). As such, we need to help future leaders set and implement goals in terms of behaviors, boundaries, alternatives, and consequences. In learning about themselves and others, adults in our principal preparation programs need to be invited to think independently, to observe, to experience, to reflect, to learn, and to dialogue.

After engaging in experiential learning, critical reflection, and rational discourse regarding their underlying assumptions about practice, future leaders for social justice, equity, and excellence need to integrate these assumptions into an informed theory of social action (i.e., action for equity). According to Mezirow (1990), "Every adult educator has the responsibility for fostering critical self-reflection and helping learners plan to take action" (p. 357).

Actually igniting reform for true excellence and the elimination of gaps in opportunity and achievement necessitates the will and the courage to do so. Educational leaders need to be attuned to the complexities of changing demographics, values, and practices, and must be, according to Sirontnik and Kimball (1996), willing "to engage in and facilitate critical and constructive inquiry" (p. 187).

In other words, they must possess a thorough knowledge and a radical critique of *what is* (e.g., present forces of domination) and a deep-seated commitment to *what ought to be* (e.g., strategies of liberation). They must be willing and able to confront and change past practices anchored in open and residual racism and class discrimination, redress social injustices, and develop enduring educational practices embodying equity. They must be willing and able to make connections, discern contradictions, and take "action against the oppressive elements of reality" (Freire, 1970, p. 74).

By critically examining the philosophical and ideological underpinnings of current issues, the educational ideas, policies, and practices that serve the interests of the dominant class while simultaneously silencing and dehumanizing "others" can be revealed. Since "oppression's causes are embedded in unquestioned norms, habits, and symbols and in the assumptions underlying institutional rules" (Young, 1990, p. 41), the purpose and nature of schooling in general, and educational processes in particular, need to be questioned and explored.

Instead, ideas, policies, and practices related to "voice" need to be examined from a critical theorist perspective (e.g., democratic processes, shared decision-making, collaboration, distributive leadership, facilitative leadership, communications, wide participation, empowerment, coalition building, activism, partnerships, alliance building, and advocacy coalitions).

Questions need to be asked. Who is included in making what decisions? What is the real purpose of site-based management? How and why does or doesn't it work? Are the themes of institutional, cultural, and personal oppression still relevant today? Who are the stakeholders? What are the organizational power arrangements? Is outrage acceptable? How can we establish structures and procedures that allow all members of the school community to participate and have a respected voice in decisions and policies that affect them?

For leadership to be authentic and effective, "purpose" ideas, policies, and practices also need to be examined. Such constructs include curriculum, content, focus, aim, expectations, priorities, the hidden curriculum, hegemony, historical patterns, and egalitarian vision. Such questions include the following: What is the purpose of basic, K-12 schooling? How is schooling carried out? Who is to be served by the educational system? What are the roles and issues facing educational leaders in our schools and in our society? How is curriculum chosen? By whom? What does it consist of? How is it delivered? What is emphasized? What is the purpose of supervision and evaluation? Do our schools have to be competitive? How do they select and sort, rate and rank? What is the message behind awards, letter grades, weighted grades, honor rolls, and class ranks?

As moral agents, leaders for social justice and equity must engage in objective ethical reasoning and be prepared to address moral dilemmas that occur daily in schools. A number of scholars have argued that we need educators who enter and remain in education not to carry on business as usual but to work for social change and social justice (Ayers, Hunt, & Quinn, 1998; Cochran-Smith, 1998; Oakes & Lipton, 1999).

Unfortunately, Rapp, Silent, and Silent (2001) found that 90 percent of educational leaders, both practitioners and professors, remained wedded to what Scott and Hart (1979) call *technical drifting*—a commitment to emphasize and act upon the technical components of one's work above the moral. The stress put on technical rather than on social, political, and moral issues is one way to avoid conflict and change.

From a critical theorist perspective, technical drifters are the opposite of leaders for equity in that they fail to validate the cultural, intellectual, and emotional identities of people from underrepresented groups; they avoid situations where their values, leadership styles, and professional goals can be challenged and dismantled; and they use their positions of power to formally and informally reaffirm their own professional choices. Their reluctance or inability to discuss philosophical values leads to avoidance and/or retreat into managerialism. As a result, moral forms of development are often jettisoned in favor of more narrowly defined agendas. This is so unfortunate.

Although no set of issues is as explosive, controversial, emotional, and threatening as moral disputes, none is more vital! When we take pains to avoid making a value judgment, we actually end up tacitly accepting the values of the status quo. We need to see the crisis in education as not primarily problems of technique, organization, and funding but as a reflection of the crisis in meaning!

As a result, "reform" ideas, policies, and practices need to be examined (e.g., accountability, testing, test bias, assessment, needs assessment, planning, school improvement, professional development, achievement, type of instruction, teaching methods, innovation, interventions, differentiation, bilingual education, school organization, school choice, vouchers, charter schools, politics, control, dropout rates, utopian ideals, resistance, reconstruction, and change).

Questions need to be asked. What is the source of the frantic demand for accountability? How accurate are the assumptions that underlie it? Who benefits and who loses when this become our primary focus? Do higher scores necessarily signal better learning? Is learning trivialized in schools? What are the politics of standardized testing? How and why are programs implemented? Which school norms are toxic? Who is helped/hurt by charter schools? How are personnel roles defined? By whom? Why?

In the same vein, "respect" ideas, policies, and practices also need to be examined, including: moral leadership, values, ethics, relationships, assumptions, beliefs, worldviews, interactions, recruitment, retention, attendance, and monitoring. Do all adults want all kids to be successful? Why/why not? If it is good for kids, will everyone embrace it? Why/why not? How can we actively reclaim, appropriate, sustain, and advance the inherent rights of equity, equality, and fairness? Are we willing and able to take risks? These and other such questions of *what is* lead us to question *what ought to be*.

According to Furman (2003) and others, educational leadership as a field is focusing more and more on what leadership is *for*. As a result, the moral purposes of educational leadership are emerging as the central focus. This perspective shift *from* what leadership is, how it is done, and by whom *toward* the purposes of leading in schools is at the heart of leadership for social justice, equity, and excellence. Why do leaders do leadership? What are the valued ends being sought? And, how can they be achieved?

Although conceiving of leadership as based in moral purpose is not new (see Foster, 1986; Greenfield, 1979; Sergiovanni 1992), what *is* new, according to Furman (2003), "is the greater emphasis on these moral purposes, a greater sense of urgency about them, and the greater recognition that much of the 'traditional' work in educational leadership hasn't helped to achieve these moral purposes" (p. 3).

Given this, certain "equity" ideas, policies, and practices need to be examined, including tracking, ability grouping, placement, gifted and talented titles, gaps in achievement, funding, gender, discipline, suspensions, honors and advanced placement (AP) courses, allocation of resources, special education labels, data, results, and teacher assignments. What do deep equity audits of the schools' institutional practices reveal? Where are the disparities? What are the causes of the achievement gaps? Are they class and/or race related? What are the complexities of poverty? How are schools funded? How are resources divided? Which students are in the AP courses? What institutionalized patterns of cultural value constitute some actors as inferior, excluded, wholly other, or simply invisible? What patterns constitute actors as peers, capable of participating on par with one another in social life? Which students get which teachers? Who benefits from the status quo? How can we create schools that are both equitable and excellent?

Likewise, "diversity" ideas, policies, and practices also need to be examined, including community, cultural inclusiveness, internalized oppression, societal discrimination, systemic and institutional racism, classism, sexism, heterosexism, ableism, deficit thinking, color blindness, historic marginalization, exclusionary processes, cultural capital, pluralism, assimilation, and enculturation.

Questions include the following: How are the themes of "control" and "cultural domination" played out throughout the history of public education? What can we learn from cross-cultural interviews, cultural plunges, and diversity panels? What does white privilege mean? What can we do to promote respectful interaction across differences? How can we grow in an awareness of the psychological effects of racism, sexism, and cultural imperialism while simultaneously not reifying group identities? What forms of communitarianism should or shouldn't we promote and why? How are race and poverty intertwined? How are disabilities socially constructed? What are the educational benefits of diversity?

If the fundamental moral imperative of schooling is to serve the best interests of all children, then leadership is needed. In conclusion, such leadership requires answers to two fundamental questions: (1) *Why* should one be a leader for social justice, equity, and excellence; and (2) *how* should one be such a leader? In answering why, leaders need to ask for whom and for what? They need to debate the value of such a pursuit despite the opposition and conflict involved in fighting such issues. Do they feel a moral calling to help every child succeed? Do they have the passion to face immense pressures under nearly impossible circumstances and still have the hope and energy necessary to transform? Are they able to accept their responsibility for being part of the problem as well as part of the solution and believe that improvement is possible? According to Larson and Murtadha (2002), leaders driven by the moral need to enact social justice for children and schools share the common belief that injustice in our schools and communities is neither natural nor inevitable.

In reflecting on these questions, leaders also need to critically examine the purpose and meaning of such leadership and the harm of *not* pursuing it? In the process, topics such as integrity, inner satisfaction, seriousness, self-respect, dignity, individual autonomy, and personal freedom might surface. Recognizing that we cannot answer these questions in a fully satisfactory and coherent way, we are still bound by intellectual honesty to explore the issues prompted by these questions and to give the best answers that we can at present. Many have to be answered practically in the course of living.

In answering *how*, leaders must first examine and understand a variety of issues from a variety of angles. Realizing that a leader's "personal formation," his or her integration of personal and professional knowledge, can provide a moral compass for navigating the complex landscape of practice, leaders need to ask radical questions that get to the root of an issue, to the root of their assumptions. The exploration of new understandings, the synthesis of new information, and the integration of these insights can lead to broader, more inclusive approaches in addressing issues of student learning, development, equity, and democracy.

Reminded by Bogotch (2002) that social justice is a social construction and "there are no fixed or predictable meanings of social justice prior to actually engaging in educational leadership practice" (p. 153), leaders committed to equity need to consciously move from empty promises and trite phrases (e.g., success for all) to justice activism. They need to oppose unfair and inequitable policies while simultaneously working to minimize their damage. They need to reject the status quo and move from rhetoric to a well-thought-through analysis of democracy that "might be" taught and practiced in schools. In the end, leaders for social justice, equity, and excellence understand that their ultimate obligation is to do what is best for children!

REFERENCES

Astin, A. W. (1993). *What matters in college? Four critical years revisited.* San Francisco, CA: Jossey-Bass.

Ayers, W., Hunt, J. A., & Quinn, T. (Eds.). (1998). *Teaching for social justice. A democracy and education reader.* New York, NY: New Press, Teachers College.

Bandura, A. (1986). *Social foundations of thought and action: A social cognitive theory.* Englewood Cliffs, NJ: Prentice Hall.

Bogotch, I. (2002). Educational leadership and social justice: Practice into theory. *Journal of School Leadership, 12*(2), 138–156.

Cochran-Smith, M. (1998). Teaching for social change: Toward a grounded theory of teacher education. In A. Hargreaves, A. Lieberman, M. Fullan, and D. Hopkins (Eds.), *The international handbook of educational change* (pp. 916–951). Dordrecht, The Netherlands: Kluwer Academic.

Dewey, J. (1938). *Experience and education.* New York, NY: Simon and Schuster.

Foster, W. (1986). *Paradigms and promises: New approaches to educational administration.* Buffalo, NY: Prometheus Books.

Freire, P. (1970). *Pedagogy of the oppressed.* New York, NY: Seabury.

Freire, P. (1998). *Pedagogy of freedom: Ethics, democracy, and civic courage.* Lanham, MD: Rowman & Littlefield.

Furman, G. (2003). The 2002 UCEA Presidential Address. *UCEA Review, XLV*(1), 1–6.

Giroux, H. (1983). *Theory and resistance in education: A pedagogy for the opposition.* Westport, CN: Bergin and Garvey.

Giroux, H. (1992). *Border crossings: Cultural workers and the politics of education.* New York, NY: Routledge.

Greenfield, T. (1979). Organizational theory as ideology. *Curriculum Inquiry, 9*(2), 97–111.

Kotter, J., & Cohen, D. (2002). *The heart of change.* Boston, MA: Harvard Business School.

Larke, P. J. (1990). Cultural diversity awareness inventory: Assessing the sensitivity of preservice teachers. *Action in Teacher Education, XII*(3), 23–30.

Larson, C., & Murtadha, K. (2002). Leadership for social justice. In J. Murphy (Ed.), *The educational leadership challenge: Redefining leadership for the 21st century* (pp. 134–161). Chicago, IL: University of Chicago.

Mezirow, J. (1990). *Fostering critical reflection in adulthood: A guide to transformative and emancipatory learning.* San Francisco, CA: Jossey-Bass.

Oakes, J., & Lipton, M. (1999). *Teaching to change the world*. Boston, MA: McGraw-Hill College.

Pajares, F. (1992). Teachers' beliefs and educational research: Cleaning up a messy construct. *Review of Educational Research, 62*(3), 307–332.

Rapp, D., Silent X, & Silent Y. (2001). The implications of raising one's voice in educational leadership doctoral programs: Women's stories of fear, retaliation, and silence. *Journal of School Leadership, 11*(4), 279–295.

Rokeach, M. (1968). *Beliefs, attitudes, and values: A theory of organization and change*. San Francisco, CA: Jossey-Bass.

Scheurich, J. & Skrla, L. (2003). *Leadership for equity and excellence: Creating high achievement classrooms, schools, and districts*. Thousand Oaks, CA: Corwin.

Scott, B. (2001, February). We should not kid ourselves: Excellence requires equity. *IDRA Newsletter*. San Antonio, TX: Intercultural Development Research Association.

Scott, W., & Hart, D. (1979). *Organizational America: Can individual freedom survive the security it promises?* Boston, MA: Houghton Mifflin.

Sergiovanni, T. (1992). *Moral leadership: Getting to the heart of school improvement*. San Francisco, CA: Jossey-Bass.

Sirontnik, K., & Kimball, K. (1996). Preparing educators for leadership: In praise of experience. *Journal of School Leadership, 6*(2), 180–201.

Skrla, L., Scheurich, J. J., Johnson, J. F., & Koschoreck. (2001). Accountability for equity: Can state policy leverage social justice? *International Journal of Leadership in Education, 4*(3), 237–260.

Sleeter, C. (1993). Forward. In C. Capper (Ed.), *Educational administration in a pluralistic society* (pp. ix–xi). Albany, NY: State University of New York.

Young, I. (1990). *Justice and the politics of difference*. Princeton, NJ: Princeton University.

Index

Note: Page numbers in *italics* refer to tables.

About the Authors

Dr. Kathleen M. Brown has been a Professor of Educational Leadership and Policy at the University of North Carolina at Chapel Hill for the past 19 years. Prior to joining the professorate, she served as a teacher and as an elementary and middle school principal in the Philadelphia/Camden, New Jersey area for more than 12 years. She has served in a number of leadership capacities in the School of Education and in the state of North Carolina including Program Chair and Coordinator, Interim Associate Dean, Strategist with the Hunt Institute, and Evaluator on the Race-to-the-Top grant. Her research interests include effective, site-based servant leadership that connects theory, practice and issues of social justice in breaking down walls and building a unified profession of culturally aware educators working toward equitable schooling for all. Dr. Brown has published over 50 refereed research articles, 15 non-refereed articles, and 20 book chapters in the field of educational leadership. She has also written and/or edited 7 books and has delivered more than 100 presentations nationally and internationally during her tenure here at UNC-Chapel Hill.

Dr. Haim Shaked is Vice President for Academic Affairs and a member of the Academic Council at Hemdat Hadarom College of Education, Netivot, Israel. As a scholar-practitioner with seventeen years of experience as school principal, his research interests include instructional leadership, system thinking in school leadership, and education reform. His book (co-author Chen Schechter, foreword by Michael Fullan) "Systems Thinking for School Leaders: Holistic Leadership for Excellence in Education" was published recently by Springer Press. His book "Leading holistically: How schools, districts, and states improve systemically" (co-editors Chen Schechter & Alan J. Daly, foreword by Michael Fullan) is about to be published by Routledge.